Economic Values and the Environment in the Developing World

Economic Values and the Environment in the Developing World

Stavros Georgiou

Senior Research Associate, Centre for Social and Economic Research on the Global Environment, University of East Anglia and University College London, UK

Dale Whittington

Professor of Environmental Sciences and Engineering and Professor of City and Regional Planning, University of North Carolina, USA

David Pearce

Professor of Environmental Economics, University College London, UK and Director, Centre for Social and Economic Research on the Global Environment, University College London and University of East Anglia, UK

Dominic Moran

Environmental Economic Advisor, Prime Minister's Department, Malaysia

Edward Elgar
Cheltenham, UK · Lyme, US

Published by
Edward Elgar Publishing Limited
8 Lansdown Place
Cheltenham
Glos GL50 2HU
UK

Edward Elgar Publishing, Inc.
1 Pinnacle Hill Road
Lyme
NH 03768
US

A catalogue record for this book is available from the British Library

Library of Congress Cataloguing-in-Publication Data

Economic values and the environment in the developing world / Stavros
    Georgiou ... [et al.].
        Includes bibliographical references and index.
            1. Environmental policy—Developing countries—Cost effectiveness.
        2. Environmental quality—Developing countries. 3. Environmental
        impact analysis—Economic aspects—Developing countries.
        4. Economic development projects—Developing countries—Cost
        effectiveness. 5. Natural resources—Valuation—Developing
        countries. I. Georgiou, Stavros G.
        HC59.72.E5E267 1997
        333.7'09172'4—dc21   96-48954
                                                                            CIP

ISBN 1 85898 500 5

Printed and bound in Great Britain by
Biddles Limited, Guildford and King's Lynn

Contents

Figures

Tables

Preface and Acknowledgements

This volume assesses the state of the art in applying economic valuation techniques to environmental problems in developing countries. It is in fulfilment of a contract between the United Nations Environment Programme (UNEP) and CSERGE, University College London and University of East Anglia. The volume outlines the available valuation techniques and surveys their application to developing country problems. It offers some guidelines and assesses the gaps in the available information. The general conclusions are that economic valuation is:

(a) extremely useful in raising the profile of the environmental aspects of development projects and policies;
(b) widespread in terms of its applications in developing countries; and
(c) generally successful in its application.

The second and third conclusions are surprising since there is a widespread view that, even if 'monetising' costs and benefits works in the developed world, it does not work in the developing world where markets are invariably managed or non-existent. Nothing could be further from the truth, as this volume shows.

We have been assisted by a community of scholars who gave freely of their time to help with the search for case studies. One reason for the perception of little activity in economic valuation in the developing world is that so much of the literature is not in journals or books. It occupies the 'grey' area of pre-publications, reports, work-in-progress, and so on. This makes it difficult to compile a comprehensive survey of what is going on. Nonetheless, we feel we have secured an extensive overview of the state of play. We are indebted to many people for sending us papers, references, and so on. and in particular to Jan Bojö, Randy Kramer, Ted McConnell, Ernst Lutz, Bill Magrath, Karl-Göran Mäler, John Dixon, Mohan Munasinghe, Kerry Smith, Giles Atkinson and Manab Chakraborty for their assistance. We also benefited from detailed comments made on the draft at a Consultative Experts Group Meeting at UNEP, Nairobi in August 1994. Our debts of gratitude are too many to list those who commented at this meeting. Finally, we are indebted to Hussein Abaza of UNEP, Nairobi, for continued encouragement and comments, Nandini Hadker for research assistance, and to Laura Fellowes for putting the volume in its final form.

1. Introduction

1.1 The Issue of Choice

Economics is about making choices. Making choices about the environment is more complex than making choices in the context of purely 'private' goods and services. Private goods are goods that when consumed by an individual, the act of consumption precludes anyone else from consuming the good as well. Private goods tend to be bought and sold in markets. Public goods have the feature that consumption tends to be 'joint' between individuals: consumption by individual A does not preclude consumption by individual B. Moreover, with public goods it is difficult, if not impossible, to exclude others from the act of consumption. To focus the issue, a private good might be an apple or a cinema seat. A public good could be clean air or improved water quality. The distinction between private and public goods can be blurred: there is a continuum of privateness and publicness.

In the environmental context, what has to be compared is a priced good (private good) and an unpriced one (public good) – as when deciding to invest in air pollution control rather than new economic output capacity. Alternatively the comparison may be between two or more unpriced public goods, for example air quality versus water quality. In this context it is necessary to impute a value to the environmental good or service. The discipline of environmental economics has developed techniques whereby such values can be constructed (see Chapter 2). In the market place individuals exercise choice by comparing their 'willingness-to-pay' (WTP) with the price of the product. They purchase the good when their WTP exceeds the price, and not otherwise. Constructing values involves finding some measure of WTP for environmental quality. This is the essence of economic valuation: it involves finding a WTP measure in circumstances where markets fail to reveal that information directly.

This 'market failure' is important for the allocation of resources within an economy. If the production of specific crops involves using agricultural technologies which give rise to soil erosion, the damage done may not be reflected in the choice of crop or technology. This may be so even where the cost of the damage is borne by the farmer growing the crops: future damage to crop productivity through soil erosion may be imperfectly reflected in choices made now. Market failure is further pronounced when the costs are borne by agents

1

other than the farmer – for example in siltation of rivers, ports and reservoirs. Failure to account for these 'external costs' gives rise to a misallocation of resources in the economy, in this case through the choice of the wrong agricultural technology. Making choices better informed to avoid this misallocation of resources involves understanding the value of the external costs, and then finding a mechanism for incorporating those values back into the original decision. Valuation may be imperfect but some valuation is almost always better than none.

The purpose of economic valuation is to reveal the true costs of using up scarce environmental resources. Choosing 'instruments' is the mechanism whereby the resulting values are reflected in decision-making. If the disposal of sewage to inland waters gives rise to loss of wellbeing, the value of that loss should be reflected in the private costs of disposing of the sewage. This might be achieved by taxing the sewage discharger; by setting some environmental standard for the effluent or the receiving waters; or by requiring the discharger to buy permits for the effluent. In general the value of the damage done does not affect the choice of instrument, that is tax, standard or permit. However it does affect the size of the tax; or the amount of pollution allowed by the permit or the standard. The virtues of economic instruments – taxes, permits and other incentive systems based on altering market signals – remain even if valuation is not carried out. But valuation is essential if the appropriate scale of the tax or strength of the regulation is to be determined.

In practice, valuation is the exception and not the rule: environmental standards are often set by criteria that incorporate some features of the valuation process. Health criteria, for example, determine many environmental standards in the developed world. Damage to human health would be an integral part of any valuation process – people will be willing to pay to avoid health risks from pollution and waste. But as there are often many other forms of damage besides health effects, using health criteria alone could impose its own distortions on resource allocation. A good deal of environmental policy is based on the concept of 'best available technology' whereby a regulator encourages the polluter to use the cleanest technology available, whilst avoiding 'excessive costs'. In many other cases, environmental standards are set without any clear or detailed rationale. Some regulations, for example, are the outcome of responses to environmental scare stories and misinformed perceptions of hazard and risk. In such circumstances, economic valuation is helpful in making explicit the criteria that have been used to form the policy. Therefore, setting environmental standards should be informed by valuation.

Valuation is relevant at all levels of public choice. In project appraisal the environmental impacts of any investment need to be estimated and compared to the other costs and benefits. Similarly in programme appraisal the value of environmental impacts needs to be integrated into the evaluation process. In policy appraisal environmental factors need to be treated on an equal footing with other costs and benefits so that sectoral priorities are not distorted. This is as important in choosing between marginal expenditures on, for example, transport and energy services, as it is in choosing between conservation and land development projects. Thus, environmental valuation should be an integral part of setting sectoral priorities, and determining the balance between conservation and development.

1.2 Whose Values Count?

Economic values are measured by individuals' WTP for benefits or their WTP to avoid costs. Typically, the values that count belong to those who are actually exercising and are affected by the choice, that is the current generation. But it is a feature of environmental costs and benefits that they often accrue to people in generations yet to come. How are their values to be counted? This is the issue of 'intergenerational incidence' of costs and benefits. Counting only the current generation's preferences biases the choice against future generations unless there is some mechanism to ensure that current generations take the interests of future generations into account. This potential bias arises because future generations are not present to have their votes counted. Whether they are present or not, future gains and losses tend to be played down in economic decision-making because of the practice of discounting. Discounting is the procedure whereby gains and losses to society are valued less the more distant they are in the future, a procedure designed to reflect the general observation that individuals simply prefer their benefits now and their costs later.

An analogous form of bias arises even within a generation: WTP is weighted by the incomes of those expressing their WTP. The economic votes of the poor count for less in the market place than the economic votes of the rich. This is the problem of 'intragenerational incidence'. Because economic votes count more the higher the income of the individual expressing the vote, economic valuation appears to be distinctly 'unfair'. This is correct up to a point, and for quite a long period in the development of economic appraisal techniques methodologies were developed for weighting the economic votes in such a way that this income bias was removed. Generally speaking they are not used now, although they could be. A practical reason why they are not used derives from the issue of what exactly one is trying to achieve by making such adjustments for varying incomes. If the aim is to reflect income distribution concerns in all decisions, then an income weighting procedure would appear to be sensible. But is it sensible to use income weighting in this way when society has more efficient means to achieve distributional goals? For example, why build income weights into an analysis of, say, a hydroelectric plant if society can correct incomes for unfairness through the tax system? There do appear, therefore, to be some sensible practical reasons for not engaging in distributional weighting. Where those reasons are not persuasive, it is possible to introduce distributional weights (see Section 1.7).

Both inter- and intragenerational bias are therefore present in the WTP criterion. There is no consensus on how to integrate inter- and intragenerational considerations into economic decision-making about the environment. While economists would typically favour the use of positive rates for discounting the future, some argue that there is no particular rationale for discounting future wellbeing. Most economists would probably focus on efficiency gains and losses in project and programme appraisal, however others favour the explicit recognition of multiple social goals or 'multi-criteria' and seek some form of calculus for trading-off between them when they conflict.

1.3 Economic Valuation and the Developing World

Discussion of economic valuation and the role of future generations' preferences may seem remote from the concerns of the developing economies. But valuation is fundamental to the notion of 'sustainable development'. If sustainable development is very loosely defined in the sense of the World Commission on Environment and Development (1987) as development that 'meets the needs of the present without compromising the ability of future generations to meet their own needs' then one must know what is and what is not a sustainable development path. It should be possible to see that a development path which ignores the environmental consequences of economic change may well be unsustainable. As environments deteriorate, so human health will suffer from environmentally-induced diseases, and long-term labour productivity may decline. Degraded environments also impose costs in terms of forgone crop output due to soil erosion; additional energy imports as biomass energy is exhausted; diverted labour time to collect water and fuelwood from increasingly distant sources, and so on. Moreover, when properly valued, investment in natural resource augmentation is often found to yield rates of economic return comparable to that earned on conventional capital investments.

Demonstrating that 'conservation pays' in economic development terms is a process that has only really just begun. But it is already possible to point out significant findings. Far from environmental and resource conservation being inimical to sustained economic development, it is in a great many cases integral to the development process.

1.4 What is Economic Valuation?

It is important to understand what is being done when economic valuation is carried out. The economic value of something is measured by the summation of many individuals' WTP for it. In turn, this WTP reflects individuals' preferences for the good in question. So, economic valuation in the environment context is about 'measuring the preferences' of people for an environmental good, or against an environmental bad. Valuation is therefore about preferences held by people. The valuation process is anthropocentric. The resulting valuations are in money terms because of the way in which preference revelation is sought – that is by asking what people are willing to pay, or by inferring their WTP through other means. Moreover, the use of money as the measuring rod permits the comparison that is required between 'environmental values' and 'development values'. The latter are expressed in money terms, either in a dollar amount or an economic rate of return. Using other units to measure environmental values would not permit the comparison with development values.

The language of economic valuation is often misleading. Studies speak of 'valuing the environment' or 'pricing the environment'. Similarly, changes in the environment affect health so it is necessary to find some valuations of changes in health status, the ultimate change being the cessation of life itself. It is commonplace to find references to 'the value of life'. Economists are apt to speak of 'the environment as commodity' which leaves them open, perhaps justifiably, to charges that this is all the environment is worth. All these terminologies generate an unfortunate image as to what the activity of economic valuation involves. What is being valued is not 'the environment' or 'life', but people's preferences for changes in the state of their environment, and their preferences for changes in the level of risk to their lives. There is no dispute that people have preferences for and against environmental change. There is no dispute that people are willing to pay to prevent or secure change: donations to conservation societies alone demonstrate this. The problem arises when this WTP is taken as *the* value of the environmental change. Many people believe that there are 'intrinsic values' in environmental assets. They are of value in themselves and are not 'of' human beings – values that exist not just because individual human beings have preferences for them. There is no reason to reject the idea of intrinsic values because the idea of measuring preferences is adopted. What is being assessed are two different things: the value of preferences people hold for or against environmental change (economic values); and the value that resides 'in' environmental assets (intrinsic values). Economic valuation is essentially about discovering the demand curve for environmental goods and services – the values of human beings for the environment. The use of money as the measuring rod is merely a convenience: it happens to be one of the limited number of ways in which people express preferences, that is through their WTP.

Once it is accepted that both forms of value exist, the issue becomes one of which values – intrinsic or economic – should inform and guide the process of making public choices. The answer is that since both values are 'legitimate', both are relevant to decision-making. Making decisions on the basis of economic values alone neither describes real world decision-making, nor would it be appropriate given that governments and the other agents involved in the development process have multiple goals. But one difference between the economic and intrinsic value approach is that economic values can, in principle, be measured. Intrinsic values cannot. If decision-makers do not feel the need for quantified assessments of gains and losses, then lack of quantification may not be an obstacle to decision-making. However it will often prove difficult to make choices between competing projects or alternative policies with differing environmental impacts, without quantitive estimates of economic values.

The practical problem with economic valuation is one of deriving credible estimates of values in contexts where there are either no apparent markets or very imperfect markets. If it is possible to derive such values, then it may be that some measures of individuals' preferences will, in any event, capture at least part of what might be called intrinsic value. This will be so if the people expressing values for the environmental change possess some concept of the intrinsic value of things. They may then be partly valuing 'on behalf' of the environment as an entity in itself.

Once again, the discussion may seem remote from the concerns of the developing countries. But it can be very important to those concerns. Many of the environmental assets that people generally feel are very important are in the developing world. Notable examples include the tropical rain forests, ecologically precious wetlands, and many of the world's endangered species. Many people feel these environmental assets have intrinsic value. They may express that view by speaking of the immorality of activities which degrade these resources, and of the 'right to existence' of tree and animal species. Such discussions are important, but at the practical level the 'development and environment' debate is frequently about the very high value placed on development in order to reduce such problems as malnourishment and underemployment. The environment will often be viewed as a luxury to be afforded later, rather than now while the struggle for development is under way. Bringing discussion of rights and intrinsic values into the policy dialogue can be counterproductive in such contexts: honouring them is perceived as forgoing the benefits of development. If, on the other hand, conservation and the sustainable use of resources can be shown to be of economic value, then the dialogue of developer and conservationist may be viewed differently – not as one of necessary opposites, but of potential complements. The remaining stage rests on finding ways for the developing world to capture the conservation benefits. If environmentalists in rich countries perceive value in conserving a rain forest in a poor country, this is of little consequence to the poor country unless there is a potential cash flow or technology transfer to be obtained.

Economic valuation is therefore a two-part process in which it is necessary to:
1.   demonstrate and measure the economic value of environmental assets – what we will call the 'demonstration process'; and

2. find ways to capture the value – the 'appropriation process'.

1.5 Total Economic Value

The economic value of environmental assets can be broken down into a set of component parts. This can be illustrated in the context of decisions about alternative land uses for a tropical forest. According to a benefit–cost rule, decisions to 'develop' a tropical forest would have to be justified by showing that the net benefits of development exceed the net benefits of 'conservation'. Development here is taken to mean some use of the forest that would be inconsistent with retention of the forest in at least approximately its natural state. Conservation could have two dimensions: preservation, which would be formally equivalent to outright non-use of the resource; and conservation which would involve limited uses of the forest consistent with retention of natural forest. The definitions are necessarily imprecise. Some people would argue, for example, that 'ecotourism' is not consistent with sustainable conservation, others that it may be. Accepting the lack of precise lines of differentiation, the benefit–cost rule would be to develop only if the development benefits minus the development costs are greater than the benefits of conservation minus the costs of conservation. Put another way, the development benefits minus both the development costs and the net conservation benefits must be positive.

Typically, development benefits and costs can be fairly readily calculated because development has attendant cash flows. For example, the benefits of timber production can be measured because market prices for timber are observable. Conservation benefits, on the other hand, are a mix of associated cash flows and 'non-market' benefits. This fact imparts two biases. The first is that the components with associated cash flows are made to appear more 'real' than those without such cash flows. There is 'misplaced concreteness': decisions are likely to be biased in favour of the development option because conservation benefits are not readily calculable. The second bias follows from the first. Unless incentives are devised whereby the non-market benefits are 'internalised' into the land use choice mechanism, conservation benefits will automatically be downgraded. Those who stand to gain from, say, timber extraction or agricultural clearance cannot consume the non-market benefits. This 'asymmetry of values' imparts a considerable bias in favour of the development option.

Conservation benefits are measured by the 'total economic value' (TEV) of the tropical forest. TEV comprises use and non-use values. Use values can in turn be broken down into direct use, indirect use and option values.

Direct use values are fairly straightforward in concept but are not necessarily easy to measure in economic terms. For example, conservation is consistent with some direct uses of tropical rain forest, including sustainable timber harvesting. Thus minor forest products output (nuts, rattan, latex, and so on) should be measurable from market and survey data, but the value of medicinal plants for the world at large is more difficult to measure.

Indirect use values correspond closely to the ecologist's concept of 'ecological functions'. For example a tropical forest might help protect watersheds, so that removing forest cover may result in water pollution and siltation, depending on the alternative use to which the forest land is put. Similarly, tropical forests 'store' carbon dioxide (CO_2). When they are burned for clearance much of the stored CO_2 is released, contributing to atmospheric warming. Tropical forests are also biologically diverse – they are home to many endemic species which may have important ecological functions.

Option value relates to the amount that individuals would be willing to pay to conserve an environmental asset for future use. That is, no use is made of it now but use may be made of it in the future. Option value is thus like an insurance premium to ensure the supply of something the availability of which would otherwise be uncertain. While there can be no presumption that option value is positive, it is likely to be so where the resource is in demand for its environmental qualities and its supply is threatened by development.

Non-use value can be sub-divided into existence and bequest values. Existence value measures WTP for preservation of an environmental asset that is not related either to current or optional use. Its intuitive basis is easy to understand because a great many people reveal their WTP for the existence of environmental assets through wildlife and other environmental charities but without taking part in the direct use of the wildlife through recreation. To some extent, this WTP may represent 'vicarious' consumption, that is consumption of wildlife videos and TV programmes, but studies suggest that this is a weak explanation for existence value. Empirical measures of existence value, obtained through questionnaire approaches (the contingent valuation method), suggest that existence value can be a substantial component of total economic value. This finding is even more pronounced where the asset is unique, suggesting high potential existence values for tropical forests and especially for luxuriant moist forests. Bequest value measures an individual's WTP to ensure that an environmental resource is preserved for the benefit of his or her descendants. Some analysts like to treat bequest value as a separate category of economic value. Others regard it as part of existence value. In empirical terms it would be hard to differentiate them.

Total economic value can therefore be expressed as:

$$\text{TEV} = \text{Direct Use Value} + \text{Indirect Use Value}$$
$$+ \text{Option Value} + \text{Existence Value} \qquad (1.1)$$

While the components of TEV are additive, care has to be taken in practice not to add competing values. There are trade-offs between different types of use value and between direct and indirect use values. For example, whereas the value of timber from selective cutting can be added to the value of minor forest products, the value of timber from clear felling cannot.

Consider how TEV can be used when analysing a land use decision. Let the options be *'con'* for conservation and *'dev'* for development. Assume the land in question is a forest area and that development involves clearing the forest. Then, on efficiency grounds, the condition for development to be socially worthwhile (ignoring time, for convenience) is:

$$(B_{dev} - C_{dev}) - (B_{con} - C_{con}) > 0 \qquad (1.2)$$

Notice that the net benefits of conservation need to be deducted from the net benefits of development for the land use change to be warranted on efficiency grounds. That is, the true 'opportunity cost' of development includes the forgone conservation benefits. Let TEV_{con} be the total economic value of the conservation option, so that the condition for land use change becomes:

$$(B_{dev} - C_{dev}) - (TEV_{con} - C_{con}) > 0 \qquad (1.3)$$

From the standpoint of society, the fact that some components of TEV_{con} may not accrue as cash flows is not relevant. It is an artefact that some goods and services are marketed while others are not. But from the standpoint of an effective decision, it is important that TEV_{con} be 'appropriated' as a cash flow or flow of real services. For example, if the decision is to conserve the forest because of non-market values in TEV_{con}, then the land owner will have to forgo the development benefits which accrue in cash terms. He cannot live off the invisible proceeds of TEV_{con}. As such, he will have little incentive to abide by any land use decision based on non-market values. This is why it is important to develop procedures for turning those values into cashable forms. Mechanisms for appropriation are discussed at length in Panayotou (1994).

1.6 Why Derive Economic Values?

There are at least five major reasons why economic valuation of environmental goods and services is important in the developing world.

1.6.1 The importance of environment in national development strategies

Environmental damage imposes costs to nations. Some of these costs produce impacts on GNP: GNP is lowered as a result of environmental damage. Other costs are not currently recorded as part of GNP, but would be if GNP accounts were modified to reflect comprehensive measures of aggregate wellbeing rather than concentrating on economic activity. Focusing on costs that are currently recorded as part of GNP, evidence is now available to show that environmental degradation results in appreciable losses of GNP. The kinds of impacts that give rise to such costs include:

1. forgone crop output due to soil erosion and air pollution;
2. forgone forestry output due to air pollution damage, soil contamination and soil erosion;
3. impairment of human health and consequent loss of labour productivity; and
4. diversion of labour and resources from high productivity uses to low productivity uses such as maintenance of buildings damaged by pollution.

The empirical investigation of these losses at a national level is in its infancy. In the case of crop losses, for example, what is required is some measure of change in the overall level of economic surpluses (consumers' and producers' surplus are measures of the extent to which WTP exceeds the actual amount paid) rather than a more straightforward estimate of crop loss valued at market prices. The impact of global warming on world agriculture is under continuing investigation using the economic surpluses approach. However, simpler approaches (as described below) based on crop responses to soil erosion and pollution have their uses too.

Soil erosion is endemic to many developing countries. Soil erodes 'naturally' but lack of investment in conservation, poor extension services, inability to raise credit and insecure land tenure all contribute to poor management of soils. A standard approach to estimating the costs of soil erosion is to estimate soil loss through the Universal Soil Loss Equation (USLE). The USLE estimates soil loss by relating it to rainfall erosivity, R; the 'erodibility' of soils, K; the slope of land, SL; a 'crop factor, C, which measures the ratio of soil loss under a given crop to that from bare soil; and conservation practice, P, ('no conservation' is measured as unity). The USLE is then:

$$\text{Soil Loss} = R * K * SL * C * P \qquad (1.4)$$

The next step is to link soil loss to crop productivity. In a study of soil loss effects in southern Mali, researchers applied the following equation to estimate the impact.

$$\text{Yield} = C^{-bz} \qquad (1.5)$$

where C is the yield on newly cleared and hence uneroded land, b is a coefficient varying with crop and slope and z is cumulative soil loss. Finally, the resulting yield reductions need to be valued. A crude approach is simply to multiply the estimated crop loss by its market price if it is a cash crop. But the impact of yield changes on farm incomes will generally be more complex than this. For example, yield reductions would reduce the requirement for weeding and harvesting. The Mali study allowed for these effects by looking at the total impact on farm budgets with and without erosion.

The procedure described above is an example of a 'dose–response' approach to valuation. The 'dose' is soil erosion, the 'response' is crop loss. Another approach would be to look at the costs of replacing the nutrients that are lost with soil erosion. Nutrient losses can be replaced with chemical fertilisers which have explicit market values.

Where it is not possible to engage in detailed assessment of the costs of resource degradation it is still useful to obtain 'best guess' calculations. In Burkina Faso estimates were made of the total amount of biomass lost each year in the form of fuelwood and vegetation. The resulting losses show up as forgone household energy (fuelwood) which can be valued at market prices for fuelwood; forgone millet and sorghum crops which can be valued at market prices; and reduced livestock yield due to fodder losses. Fuelwood losses amount to some 47 CFAF billion (1990 US$ 156 million), livestock 10 CFAF billion (1990 US$ 33 million), and cereal losses a further 15 CFAF billion (1990 US$ 50 million). The grand total amounts to some 9 per cent of Burkina Faso GNP. It cannot be deduced from this that Burkina Faso's GNP is 9 per cent less than it otherwise would be. This is because resources would have to be expended in order to rehabilitate eroded areas and to prevent further damage. But if the resources required are small, then the 9 per cent figure is a ballpark estimate of the direct loss to Burkina Faso.

Provided they are credible, national environmental damage cost estimates can play a useful role in assessing development priorities. Because environmental damage costs do not show up explicitly in measures of national product, planners have no obvious incentive to treat environmental damage as a priority in development plans. Increasingly, however, environment is entering into development plans as the GNP costs of degradation are being shown to be significant and sometimes very substantial. Arguments of this kind are particularly appropriate at the level of macroeconomic management of the economy: it may be more important that the Ministry of Finance appreciates the costs of environmental degradation than that the Ministry of the Environment does.

1.6.2 Modifying the national accounts
Macroeconomic management makes extensive use of the national economic accounts which record monetary flows and transactions within the economy. The primary purpose of the accounts is to record economic activity, rather than to attempt to measure aggregate wellbeing in the nation. None the less, national accounts are widely used to indicate wellbeing and rates of change in national

aggregates such as GNP are widely construed as measures of 'development'. Whether the accounts are designed to record economic activity or measure wellbeing, or both, they are deficient in respect of their treatment of environment. Economic activity involves the use of materials and energy resources, which having been transformed into goods and services, sooner or later become waste products. Any measure of economic activity which ignores these materials and energy flows will fail to record important activities which affect the sustainability of the economic activity. In the same way, any measure of wellbeing which ignores the resource and energy flows will fail to measure 'sustainable wellbeing'. For these reasons, there is now widespread consensus that the national accounts need to be modified at least with respect to the way in which environmental 'stocks' and 'flows' are recorded.

Materials and energy flows begin at the point of extraction, harvest or use of natural resources. They terminate at the point where goods and resources become waste products, that is emissions to air, discharges to water, or solid waste to land or sea. Logically, then, GNP needs to be modified to account for:

1. any depreciation of natural capital stocks, in the same way that net national income = gross national income less estimated depreciation on man-made capital. This is a measure of the 'draw down' of natural capital; and
2. any losses accruing to human wellbeing from the extraction, processing and disposal of materials and energy to receiving environments.

Both adjustments involve economic valuation. The first adjustment involves a valuation of the natural capital stock; the second involves valuation of such things as health impairment, pollution damage to buildings, crops and trees, aesthetic and recreational losses and other forms of 'psychic' damage. National accountants have not agreed how best to make the appropriate adjustments.

Depreciation of stocks of natural capital is relevant when one is interested in some measure of sustainable income, that is the income that a nation can receive without running down its capital base. In the conventional accounts this is partly accounted for by estimating net national product (NNP) which is defined as:

$$NNP = GNP - D_k \qquad (1.6)$$

where D_k is the depreciation on man-made capital (machines, roads, buildings, and so on). The further adjustment that is required is:

$$NNP = GNP - D_k - D_n \qquad (1.7)$$

where D_n is the depreciation of environmental assets.

There is a clear role for economic valuation in establishing modified national income accounts.

1.6.3 Setting national and sectoral priorities

Information on the economic value of policy changes can greatly assist government in setting policy and sectoral priorities. Estimating damage or benefit figures alone will not be sufficient for this process. It is necessary to compare the benefits of a policy with its costs. The presence of net benefits is sufficient to establish that existing or planned policy is potentially worthwhile. But if benefits are less than costs, it can be inferred that resources should not be devoted on such a scale to the particular goal. This general requirement to review sectoral priorities in terms of benefits and costs has perhaps even greater force in the developing world where government income is at a premium. Indeed, this has always been one of the motives underlying the development of benefit–cost valuation techniques for developing countries. Despite this, sectoral benefit–cost techniques have only been used in fairly limited ways in the developed world, and hardly at all in the developing world. Although there are a great many benefit–cost studies of specific policies in both developed and developing countries, few exist for establishing the worth of overall sectoral expenditures.

In the real world of political decision-making, priorities are rarely set by reference to measures of costs and benefits. Estimates of costs and benefits have perhaps the greatest influence over policy in the United States. Outside of the US very little actual influence has been exerted by benefit–cost analysis. In part this reflects lack of understanding of the techniques involved, and the fact that decision-makers have multiple criteria for deciding on policies. Policies are not necessarily chosen on a rational basis from the social standpoint: chance, favouritism, patronage, whim and corruption may be important factors. Benefit and damage estimation are therefore likely to be part of a wider package of criteria used in policy formation, other criteria including distributional concerns, human health, the quality of environmental impact and the sustainability of resource use.

1.6.4 Project, programme and policy evaluation

The traditional role for environmental damage and benefit estimation is in project appraisal. The main manuals that have influenced theoretical and practical work in economic project assessment have not, however, addressed environmental issues. Issues relating to the treatment of environmental factors are not, for example, discussed at all in the main project appraisal technical manuals, for example Little and Mirrlees (1974); Squire and van der Tak (1975); UNIDO (1972); and Gittinger (1982). In contrast, assessing environmental impacts has been the subject of a wholly separate set of procedures known as Environmental Impact Assessment (EIA), or Environmental Assessment (EA).

EA is important in drawing decision-makers' attention to the many forms of environmental impact that may occur as a result of a result of a project or policy. To some extent EA also permits an assessment of the importance of impacts. The main problem, however, is that EA tends to be pursued either as an adjunct to conventional economic appraisal, or as a precursor. In neither case is EA integrated into economic appraisal.

Extending project appraisal to account for environmental impacts, or to the assessment of conservation projects presents no conceptual problem for benefit–cost approaches. Costs and benefits associated with environmental impacts are often not fully incorporated into market prices, which are then said to be 'distorted'. The typical benefit–cost assessment (BCA) calculates measured benefits and costs and converts them into an economic rate of return (ERR). In this process, market prices are adjusted for distortions, a process known as shadow pricing. The necessity for shadow pricing tends to arise more from the fact that environmental costs and benefits lack associated markets altogether rather than from the existence of distorted markets. Indeed, economic valuation of environmental impacts is essentially a matter of shadow pricing.

In order to focus on the environment, the traditional BCA rule for the potential acceptance of a project can be expressed as:

$$\Sigma_t (B_t - C_t - E_t).\ (1 + r)^{-t} > 0 \qquad\qquad (1.8)$$

where B_t is non–environmental benefit at time t, C_t is non-environmental cost, r is the discount rate, and E_t is environmental cost. In the case of environmental benefits the term $- E_t$ becomes $- (- E_t)$, that is $+ E_t$. Economic valuation is concerned with the monetary measurement of E_t in this inequality. Environmental issues do, however, raise a further problem, namely the selection of r, the discount rate, in the above inequality.

It is important that the environmental implications of both projects and programmes should be evaluated, and the overall return to a development programme should be assessed with reference to the inclusion of environmental enhancement components, for example tree planting, soil conservation, water supply, and so on. In programme analysis ERRs should be estimated wherever possible, especially where the intermixing of policy changes and projects is liable to make ERRs higher than if projects were being evaluated individually.

Choice of technology is often an important issue in development programmes. A given development objective may be met by selecting technology from a range of options. For example, the programme objective of meeting a given increase in electricity demand involves selecting methods of electricity generation that contribute to the overall objective of meeting demand at least cost. Whereas least cost power system planning has typically been couched in terms of the private costs of generation and distribution, environmental considerations require that the criterion be modified to become least 'social' cost, that is including valuations of the environmental impacts of different energy technologies.

Valuation is also important for implementation of the 'Polluter Pays Principle' (PPP). PPP requires that those emitting damaging wastes to the environment should bear the costs of avoiding that damage, or of reducing damage to acceptable limits according to national environmental standards. The PPP does not necessarily require that environmental damage be valued in monetary terms – simply that whatever the cost of achieving the national standard, that cost should, in the first instance, be borne by the emitter of waste. Some or all of the emitter's increased costs may then be passed on to the consumer.

Environmental standards are set by regulatory agencies on behalf of the population. Regulatory agencies should set standards such that the costs borne by the emitter and consumer in meeting the standard are equal to the minimum estimated value of the damage caused by the emissions being controlled. The costs borne by the emitter and the consumer can therefore be thought of as a form of valuation.

The PPP is therefore consistent with traditional standard setting via 'command and control' policies. It is not essential for the general PPP to be implemented via taxation or some other form of 'economic instrument' (tradeable permit, product charge, tax-subsidy, and so on). However, economic instruments such as charges and taxes have many attractions over command and control policies. If economic instruments are used it is fundamental they should be at least proportional to damage done. Valuation therefore becomes important in giving guidance to setting environmental 'prices' in the form of taxes, charges or tradeable permits.

1.6.5 Economic Valuation and Sustainable Development

The need for economic valuation of environmental impacts and of environmental assets arises quite independently from the definition of sustainable development. Simply pursuing efficient policies and investing in efficient projects and programmes requires valuation to be pursued as long as it is credible. Therefore valuation is required even at the most general level of intergenerational concern. When transfers of resources are to be made between generations – with the current generation sacrificing for the future, or future benefits being lost for the sake of present gain – it becomes essential to know what is being sacrificed and how much is being surrendered. It is not necessary, therefore, to invoke the philosophy of sustainable development (however it is defined), to justify focusing on economic valuation in the context of development.

However, if one or more definitions of sustainable development are to be espoused, the role of economic valuation needs to be investigated. An efficient use of resources need not be a sustainable one. The optimal rate at which an exhaustible resource should be depleted, for example, still requires that the rate of use is positive. In the absence of repeated discoveries of further identical resources, the resource must be exhausted eventually. Every unit of use today is at the cost of a forgone unit tomorrow. A significant example of an activity that impairs the welfare of future generations is global warming. 'Sustainability' therefore implies maintaining the level of human wellbeing so that it might improve or at least stay approximately the same over time. Interpreted this way, sustainable development becomes equivalent to a requirement that wellbeing does not decline through time. Once the goal of sustainable development is adopted, the requirement for valuation is somewhat greater than when considering efficiency alone. It becomes necessary to measure human wellbeing in order to establish that it does not decline through time. Since environmental assets contribute to wellbeing it is necessary to measure preferences for and against environmental change.

Non-economic indicators may also provide information about the conditions for achieving sustainable development. For example, computations of the carrying capacity of natural environments could act as early warnings of non–survivability. Other physical measures could include assessments of the rate of resource use relative to the rate of resource regeneration, and the rate of waste emissions relative to the assimilative capacity of the environment. It may be therefore that some light will be shed on sustainability by non-economic approaches, especially if they can be developed to include measures of stress and shock to natural resource systems.

The literature on environmental economics tends to suggest that the clues to sustainability lie in the quantity and quality of a nation's capital stock. Part of the intuition here is that nations are like corporations. No corporation would regard itself as sustainable if it used up its capital resources to fund its sales and profits expansion. As long as capital assets are at least intact, and preferably growing, any profit or income earned can be regarded as 'sustainable'. Similarly at a national level, sustainable growth and development cannot be achieved if capital assets are declining. Indeed, some economic growth models suggest strongly that if capital assets are kept intact, one concept of intergenerational equity – that of equalising real consumption per capita – can be achieved providing population growth does not outstrip the rate of technological change. (This is a big caveat since it is likely to be met in rich countries but not in very poor countries).

If a condition for achieving sustainable development is that capital stocks must be kept intact, the problem of how to tell whether a nation is 'on' or 'off' a sustainable development path is partially resolved. It is not necessary to observe real levels of wellbeing as such, as one can instead look at the underlying condition and size of the capital stock. Unfortunately, while this approach solves one problem it raises many others. First, it is necessary to know what it is that counts as capital. Second, it has to be measurable, otherwise 'constancy' of capital cannot be tested (constancy throughout should be read as 'constant or increasing').

Defining and measuring natural capital should become part of the national accounting processes. The primary condition for sustainable development would then be that the aggregate stock of capital should not decline. Put another way, depreciation on the capital stock should not exceed the rate of new investment in capital assets.

But how is the capital stock to be measured? For some economies heavily dependent on one or two natural resources it may be possible to use a physical indicator of reserves or available stocks. But for the vast majority of countries it will be necessary to find a measuring rod for capital. Typically that means money units – that is it becomes necessary to value capital, including environmental capital. Valuation and sustainable development are again intricately linked. How far this link matters depends on how likely development paths are to be unsustainable, and of course, on the value judgement that sustainability 'matters'.

If securing sustainable development depends on monitoring and measuring aggregate capital stocks and not allowing them to decline, there need be no particular role for environmental protection in sustainable development. Environmental assets could decline in quantity as long as depreciation in these assets was offset by investment in other man-made assets or human capital. But even if this view of sustainability is accepted, valuation is still central to the process. For it is not possible to know whether sufficient offsetting investment has taken place unless there is some measure of the rate of depreciation on natural assets and their forgone economic rate of return. Of course one may still make a special case for the environment. The acceptability of 'running down' environmental assets provided other assets are built up will depend on relative valuations and judgements based on other measures of sustainability, as well as moral views about destroying the environment.

Discussing sustainable development in broad terms risks giving the impression that philosophers and economists fiddle while the Rome of under-development burns. It is important to remember the sustainable development debate does not undermine immediate needs for development, or the importance of targeting policies to improve conditions for the most vulnerable in society. However this will become a risk if sustainable development is used to justify large sacrifices of real income and wellbeing now for very long term gains that are highly uncertain. Eliciting economic values can help guard against such decisions by showing, as far as possible, where and when environmental protection yields the highest returns.

1.7 Economic Valuation and Income Distribution

Section 1.2 raised the issue of the relationship between WTP and income. In general, a person with a high income will be WTP more for environmental assets than a person on a low income. Now consider an example of, say, a rain forest which is utilised by local people for fuel, wildmeat, and other forest products. It is a candidate for protection because of its biological diversity value, but this value resides mainly with people outside the country in question, for example in Europe or North America. If we compare the WTP of local people to keep the forest for their own use with the WTP of foreigners wanting to visit the forest or simply preserve it for its existence value, the chances are that the latter WTP will greatly exceed the former simply because of the income difference. Should the forest be conserved according to the wishes of foreigners, or left to local societies to use as they see fit? The comparison of WTPs suggests it should be conserved, but this decision appears to be unfairly influenced by the distribution of income between the local and foreign people.

There are two reactions to such an outcome. The first is to remember that the criterion of economic efficiency is usually only one of several criteria that might be relevant for setting policy. The point of the valuation in this case would be to test the WTP of foreigners so that some of that WTP can be 'captured' by local people. Thus measuring the WTP of foreigners can be used to set charges for tourists wanting to visit the forest. The revenues collected can be used to compensate the local people for any forgone benefits, or to create new assets that substitute for those in the forest. In this way both the conservation objective and the distributional objective are served: the local people are no worse off (and indeed could be far better off), and the forest is conserved for sustainable uses such as eco–tourism. Obviously, such a policy has to be handled cautiously and – critically – its success is dependent on both finding an appropriation mechanism and making sure that those who lose initially are compensated.

The second reaction to the perceived unfairness of comparing WTPs of people with different incomes is to modify the comparison of the WTPs in some way that lessens the effect of income. 'Equity weights' of this kind are commonly expressed in terms of the 'social value' of an extra unit of income accruing to individuals in specified groups or income classes. If an equity weight of zero were assigned to an individual, this would be equivalent to not giving him standing in the analysis. In practice, economists have generally proposed equity weighting schemes based on a functional relationship between an individual's utility or wellbeing (U) and his income (Y).

Two commonly proposed functional forms are:

$$dU/dY = Y^a \quad \text{where } a < 0 \tag{1.9}$$

$$dU/dY = e^{(Y/Y_0)} \tag{1.10}$$

where Y_0 is the mean income of the population.

The derivative of the chosen income–utility function evaluated at a particular income level is termed the 'equity weight'. For example, suppose a person below a certain income level is assigned an equity weight of 2 and his WTP for a policy alternative is $100. Using an equity weighting procedure, his adjusted WTP for the policy alternative would be $200.

If the analyst is uncertain what values to use for equity weights, one approach is to treat the weights as unknowns and solve for the values that would make one policy just as attractive as an alternative policy. For example, suppose that there are only two groups of affected individuals: the poor and everyone else. An equity weight, v_{poor}, is required to increase the social value of benefits to the poor, and the weight for other groups is simply equal to one. Let the summation of the WTP of poor individuals for policy j be:

$$WTP_{poor,j} = B_{poor,j} \qquad (1.11)$$

and the summation of the WTP of everyone else for policy j be:

$$WTP_{nonpoor,j} = B_{nonpoor,j} \qquad (1.12)$$

If policy alternatives 1 and 2 were equally attractive in terms of an economic efficiency criterion, this would imply that:

$$v_{poor} B_{poor,1} + B_{nonpoor,1} = v_{poor} B_{poor,2} + B_{nonpoor,2} \qquad (1.13)$$

Solving for v_{poor} yields:

$$v_{poor} = (B_{nonpoor,2} - B_{nonpoor,1}) / (B_{poor,1} - B_{poor,2}) \qquad (1.14)$$

If the values of $B_{poor,1}$, $B_{poor,2}$, $B_{nonpoor,1}$, and $B_{nonpoor,2}$ were known, then the last equation could be solved for a value of v_{poor} that would make the two policy alternatives equally attractive. Depending on the values of $B_{poor,1}$, $B_{poor,2}$, $B_{nonpoor,1}$, and $B_{nonpoor,2}$, higher or lower values of v_{poor} would favour one policy alternative or the other. This type of 'break-even analysis' can be quite useful if the analyst is uncertain of the exact value of an equity weight, but is confident that it is above or below a certain value, or lies within a certain range.

Equity weighting schemes of various types have been proposed by economists and policy analysts for over thirty years, but they have rarely been used in practice. Nor in our judgement is it likely that they will be used in the future. The reason for this lack of acceptance is not hard to discern: neither decision-makers nor the public are interested in the aggregate measures that result from equity weighting procedures. This largely because there is no political consensus (in any society) on how such equity weights should be determined. More broadly, such equity weights rarely capture the ethical complexity of policy choices, and thus do not help policy makers or the public think carefully or creatively about the attractiveness of policy alternatives.

REFERENCES

Gittinger, J. P. (1982), *Economic Analysis of Agricultural Projects*, Baltimore: Johns Hopkins University Press.

Little, I. and Mirrlees, J. (1974), *Project Appraisal and Planning for Developing Countries*, London: Heinemann.

Panayotou, T. (1994), *Financing Mechanisms for Environmental Investments and Sustainable Development*, Harvard: Harvard Institute for International Development, mimeo.

Squire, L. and van der Tak, H. (1975), *Economic Analysis of Projects*, Baltimore: Johns Hopkins University Press.

UNIDO (1972), *Guidelines for Project Evaluation*, Vienna: UNIDO.

World Commission on Environment and Development (1987), *Our Common Future*, London: Oxford University Press.

2. Economic Valuation Methodology

2.1 Introduction

In this chapter, we discuss the principle techniques for assigning economic values to non-market goods and services. There is both great interest and great scepticism in attempts to put monetary values on environmental goods and services – to quantify what many people believe is best left unquantified. The interest in valuation techniques arises partly from concern that efforts to protect and improve the environment should be cost effective and increase human wellbeing. The scepticism has two somewhat different sources. First, some people feel that it would be useful to know the economic value of environmental goods and services, but do not believe that it is possible to measure it accurately. Second, others feel that it is possible to measure economic value, but do not believe that this is relevant information for making public decisions regarding the environment.

These differences in perspective result in the four categories depicted in Table 2.1. Individuals in cell A believe that it is possible to develop reasonable estimates of the economic value of environmental goods and services, and that such information is useful for policy making. We would throw our lot in with individuals in this category. Individuals in cell B believe that estimates of economic value would be useful if they were available, but feel it is unlikely that current measurement techniques are sufficiently accurate and reliable to generate usable information for policy purposes. We are sympathetic with this perspective; many environmental valuation problems pose thorny methodological and theoretical difficulties. But our view is that individuals in cell B should be convinced that valuation techniques have advanced to the point where it is often worth the effort to try to estimate economic values.

Individuals in cell C do not doubt that economists can assign values to environmental goods and services, but do not believe that this is relevant or useful information for setting environmental policy. Individuals in cell D do not believe economists can estimate economic values accurately, but they do not consider this much of a problem because, like individuals in cell C, they do not think this information is of much use. It may be impossible to convince anyone in cell D to change their mind about either the feasibility of environmental valuation techniques or the utility of information on economic values. It is important to understand that economists tend *not* to believe that information on individuals' preference satisfaction is the only relevant information on which to base environmental policy decisions. But we do believe that human wellbeing matters and that people are usually the best judges of their own wellbeing. Given this, it makes sense to measure the criterion of preference satisfaction (that is economic efficiency) as best we can.

Table 2.1 Perspectives on measuring economic values of environmental goods

	Economic values of environmental goods and services:	
Economic values of environmental goods and services are:	Can be measured accurately and reliably	Cannot be measured accurately and reliably
Useful for policy making	Cell A	Cell B
Not useful for policy making	Cell C	Cell D

2.2 Economic Valuation and the Measurement of Wellbeing

The decision about the appropriate measure of economic wellbeing depends primarily on what the measure is to be used for. Policy makers can ask a range of different questions, so the welfare measure will have to be tailored appropriately. Policy makers may wish to select only policies which make at least one person better off, and nobody worse off (the so-called 'Pareto criterion'). This approach avoids the problem of comparing the unobservable wellbeing of different individuals, but in so doing faces the very strong possibility that no policy will actually exist where nobody faces net costs. This is especially likely when the policy will affect large numbers of people in different areas and sectors.

Policy makers might then choose a somewhat weaker decision rule which says that a policy is acceptable so long as those who gain could compensate those who lose, and still be better off. This 'Hicks–Kaldor' compensation test (Hicks, 1939; Kaldor, 1939) is termed a 'potential' Pareto improvement criterion. The question then becomes whether it is thought that compensation should actually be paid. If so, the government takes the role of levying taxes and making transfer payments between gainers and losers. If compensation is not deemed appropriate, this is equivalent to assuming that wellbeing, and changes in wellbeing, can be compared between and added up across individuals. This principle underlies conventional benefit–cost analysis.

The task that remains is then to measure changes in individuals' wellbeing. Wellbeing can be affected by changes in prices (both implicit and explicit) and/or qualities of goods and services. If goods and services are broadly substitutable, then trade-offs can be made and values established. Money prices can, at least in theory, constitute marginal values since they represent the quantities of marketed goods and services which must be given up when one unit of some particular good or service is purchased and consumed.

Accepting money as a measure of value, the rate at which a particular individual is prepared to trade-off goods and services against one another is equal to that individual's own maximum willingness-to-pay (WTP) for the good or service in question. Then the value of a change in the price or quality of a good or service is the total WTP for the change. More technically, it is the payment required to make an individual indifferent to a choice between the situation before the change and the situation after the change. This payment can be positive or negative depending on whether the individual gains or loses from the change. Negative payments are referred to as the individual's willingness-to-accept (WTA) compensation for the change.

The payment required to make a person indifferent to a change can be evaluated from the position before the change or after. When evaluating the payment before the change, the payment is called the 'compensating variation' of the change. In the case of change that would increase a person's wellbeing, this is the maximum payment an individual could make and still be as well off after the change as they were before. For a detrimental change, it is the minimum amount that would be needed to be paid to the individual for his or her wellbeing to be as great after the change as before. If the payment is evaluated from the position after the change, it is called the 'equivalent variation'. This is the minimum amount of money which would have to be given to the individual for them to be willing to forego the change. Alternatively, it is the maximum they would be willing to give up (pay) to avoid some detrimental change.

The important thing to note is that both compensating and equivalent variation hold some level of wellbeing constant when the value of a change is being estimated. But this is not true for the most easily observed measure of WTP, the market demand curve. This is because moving up or down a person's demand curve will usually result in 'income effects' – similar to changing the level of their income. However it is the effects on consumption from changing prices or qualities – the 'substitution effects' which are relevant for wellbeing measurement. In other words, estimating changes in wellbeing from ordinary demand curves will result in values which are biased by the inclusion of this income factor. The change in wellbeing, estimated from ordinary demand curves, is called the 'consumer's surplus', and is given by the area under the ordinary (Marshallian) demand curve between the change in prices.

Willig (1976) has argued persuasively that, in most cases, income effects are going to be so small that the difference between the theoretically correct compensating/equivalent variation estimates and those based on consumer's surplus will not be significant. However, income effects might well be significant for the case of environmental changes resulting in the *total* destruction or creation of some natural resource. Moreover, since Willig's article, advances have been made in the area of welfare estimation, and more precise methods do now exist for estimating compensating or equivalent variation. In what follows, the estimation methods described will in general be those appropriate for calculating compensating and equivalent variation.

2.3 Types of Economic Value

The monetary measure of a change in an individual's wellbeing due to a change in environmental quality is called the total economic value (TEV) of the change. It is important to understand that it is not environmental quality itself that is being measured, but people's preferences for that quality. Valuation is therefore anthropocentric in that it relates to preferences held by people, and the economic value of something is established by an actual or hypothetical exchange transaction.

Table 2.2 An economic taxonomy for environmental resource valuation

Total Economic Value				
Use Values			Non-Use Values	
Direct Use Value	Indirect Use Value	Option Value	Bequest Value	Existence Value
Outputs directly consumable	Functional benefits	Future direct and indirect values	Use and Non-Use value of environmental legacy	Value from knowledge of continued existence
Food, biomass, recreation, health	Flood control, storm protection, nutrient cycles	Biodiversity, conserved habitats	Habitats, prevention of irreversible change	Habitats, species, genetic, ecosystem

Source: Pearce *et al.* (1992)

The TEV of a resource can be disaggregated into use value (UV) and non-use value (NUV), also called 'passive use value'. Use values can be direct use values (DUV), indirect use value (IUV) and option value (OV). Direct use values are derived when an individual makes actual use of a facility, for example visiting a recreation area to go fishing. Indirect use values arise from the natural functioning of ecosystems, such as storm protection provided by trees. Option value is an individual's WTP for the option of using an asset at some future date.

NUV has proved to be both difficult to define and measure. It can be subdivided into existence value (XV), which measures WTP for a resource for some 'moral', altruistic or other reason and is unrelated to current or future use; and bequest value (BV), which measures an individual's WTP to ensure that his or her heirs will be able to use a resource in the future. So,

$$TEV = UV + NUV = (DUV + IUV + OV) + (XV + BV) \qquad (2.1)$$

Table 2.2 presents an economic taxonomy for environmental resource valuation.

2.4 Willingness-to-Pay versus Willingness-to-Accept

Valuation provides a link between physical change to the environment (for example damage) and its re-expression in terms of WTP or WTA. A number of approaches are available for determining the economic values of environmental change. First, the question arises of which measure of welfare change – WTP or WTA – should be used. Until recently, it was assumed that in most practical situations, the difference between the two measures would be small so long as there was an absence of strong income effects (Willig, 1976).

However, a substantial body of empirical evidence now exists to provide convincing evidence that WTA measures substantially exceed those based on WTP (see, for instance, Kahneman, Knetsch and Thaler, 1990, for a review). Despite initial doubts, the difference between WTP and WTA measures has proved to be extremely robust in a wide variety of experiments, and appears to reflect a real difference in individuals' valuation of a policy change depending on how the policy is 'framed' or the individual's 'reference point' (Kahneman and Tversky, 1979; Tversky and Kahneman, 1981). Individuals seem to attach much more weight (or value) to losses from this reference point than they do to gains, that is the loss of £100 from current income will generally be perceived to be much worse than a gain of £100 is perceived to be a benefit. This is not simply because of the declining marginal utility of income, that is the additional satisfaction from an extra £1 of income is assumed to decline as income grows. Instead, the 'utility function' – the way in which individuals' satisfaction varies with the quantity of commodities consumed – appears to be 'kinked' at the reference point.

This finding has a number of important implications (see Knetsch, 1990). In particular, the decision whether to use WTP or WTA for benefits estimation could in many cases take on great practical importance because the losses associated with changes in the status quo – or the reference point – would weigh much more heavily than corresponding gains. Individuals tend to view compensation for a loss as two separate events: (1) a loss (which they greatly dislike); and (2) a money payment which is perceived as a gain from their new (lower) reference point. Policy measures that mitigate or reduce losses may thus be more desirable than those that allow the damage to occur and then compensate the individuals affected.

Hanemann (1991) has offered another explanation for the divergence between WTP and WTA measures of economic value. He has shown that such wide differences can be consistent with economic theory when there are few or poor substitutes for the goods or services in question. This condition is likely to be true for some environmental goods. Others have argued that disparities can still be observed for goods which do not share the necessary characteristics (for example Dubourg *et al.*, 1994). Controversy still surrounds this issue, and good economic analysis requires good professional judgement on the question of whether to use WTP or WTA measures of economic value.

2.5 Valuation Techniques

The valuation task is to determine how much better or worse off individuals are (or would be) as a result of a change in environmental quality. As mentioned earlier, economists define the value of a change in terms of how much of something else an individual is willing to give up to get this change (or how much they would accept in order to permit the change to occur). But how can an analyst ever know what an individual would be willing to give up (or to pay) in order to have a specified change in environmental quality? There are five broad ways to try to address this question.

First, one could experiment. If an analyst wanted to know how much people would value a potential new national park, the park could be created and an entrance fee could be charged. An analyst could then observe how many people actually used the park, in effect exchanging money for the recreation and aesthetic experience of visiting the park. Or if an analyst wanted to know how much people would be willing to pay to live in a city with improved air quality, an experiment could be conducted in which air quality standards and property taxes would be raised in some cities and not in others. The analyst could then see how many people found it worthwhile to move to cities with improved air quality and higher taxes. In practice, of course, such large scale experiments of this kind are exceedingly difficult to design and politically impossible to implement. Other ways must be used to determine how people value environmental goods and services.

A second approach is simply to ask people how much they would be willing to give up (that is how much they would be willing to pay) to have a specified environmental quality improvement happen. This is known as the 'contingent valuation method' and is a 'stated preferences' technique. It is also termed the 'direct approach' to valuation because people are directly asked to state or reveal their preferences. If people were able to understand clearly the change in environmental quality being offered, and answered truthfully, this direct approach would be ideal. It measures precisely what the analyst wants to know – the individual's strength of preference for the proposed change – and could be used not only for non-market goods and services, but market goods as well. There are several practical difficulties with this approach, but the central problem is whether the intentions people indicate *ex ante* (before the change) will accurately describe their behaviour *ex post* (after the change) when people face no penalty or cost associated with a discrepancy between the two. Two other 'stated preference' techniques related to the contingent valuation method are 'contingent ranking' and 'conjoint analysis'.

Economists have been very concerned that stated intentions will not correspond to behaviour, and have thus traditionally used a third approach for measuring the value of non-market goods: surrogate markets. To use this technique, economists try to find a good or service that is sold in markets and is related to or 'bundled with' the non-market service. In this situation the individual may reveal his or her preferences for both the market and non-market service when he or she purchases the market good. For example, when making a decision on what house to buy or apartment to rent, an individual may consider many factors such as the size and age of the house, its proximity to schools, shopping, and place of employment – and perhaps the air quality in the neighbourhood. An estimate of the value of improved air quality can be 'recovered' from a careful analysis of such transactions in the housing market. This 'surrogate market' method is known as the 'hedonic property value model'. Other surrogate market techniques include, the travel cost model, the hedonic wage model and the avertive behaviour model.

All of these surrogate market methods rely on the 'behavioral trail' left by individuals as they make actual decisions that affect their lives. Individuals reveal their preferences through their actual behaviour. The estimates obtained of the value of non–market goods are based on information on what people actually did and on a set of maintained assumptions about why they did them – not what people said they would do under a set of hypothetical conditions.

This third approach is not, however, without disadvantages. For example, it is not feasible to use surrogate market methods to estimate the value of a new good or service, or of a change in environmental quality outside of current experience because no situations exist where people have been offered this new level of environmental quality and have revealed their preferences for it. Even if the non-market good or service has been available, there may never have been any significant variation in its quality, so that everyone in a particular area must automatically 'consume' the same amount of it. In such a case, it is impossible to infer how people in the area would respond to a change in quality. Finally, to implement any of the surrogate market methods, the analyst must impose a theoretical framework in order to interpret the information on individuals' decisions within a valuation context. The estimates of value derived will thus depend upon a series of assumptions that remain largely untested.

A fourth approach is available. For changes in environmental quality that reduce individuals' wellbeing, an analyst can attempt to determine the damages an individual will suffer or has suffered. A deterioration in environmental quality could cause a loss of productive assets or loss in earning power. An individual could be 'made well' or restored to their initial state of wellbeing by being compensated in money or other goods or services by the amount of the loss. This is termed the 'conventional market' or 'damage function' approach.

The conventional market and surrogate market techniques are termed 'indirect' valuation approaches because neither relies on people's direct answers to questions about how much they would be willing to pay (or accept) to have a change in environmental quality occur.

The fifth approach to obtaining estimates of the value of environmental goods and services takes a somewhat different tack. Rather than developing new estimates of value for the environmental good or service of interest, the analyst finds estimates of value for the same or similar good or service in other locations, and then transfers these estimates – perhaps after some adjustment to the location of interest. The analyst can transfer estimates of value developed using any of the other approaches described above. This is known as the 'benefit transfer' approach.

2.6 Stated Preference Approaches – Contingent Valuation

Stated preference valuation techniques are generally based on some form of questionnaire. In contingent valuation (CV) studies, people are asked directly to state, or are asked a question that will reveal what they are willing to pay to gain an improvement in the provision of a good or service, or to avoid a detrimental change in the provision of a good or service. Alternatively (or additionally) they may be asked what they are willing to accept to forego an improvement, or tolerate a detrimental change. The situation the respondent is asked to value is hypothetical (hence, 'contingent'), although respondents are assumed to behave as if they were in a real market. Structured questions can be devised involving 'yes/no' answers to questions regarding the acceptability of a proposal at a specified price. Econometric techniques are then used on the survey results to find the mean value of WTP.

There are three basic parts to most CV survey instruments. First, a hypothetical description (scenario) of the terms under which the good or service is to be offered is presented to the respondent. Information is provided on the quality and reliability of provision, its timing and logistics, and the method of payment. Often the good needs to be described in the overall context of the general class of environmental goods under consideration.

Second, the respondent is asked questions to determine how much he or she would value a good or service if confronted with the opportunity to obtain it under the specified terms and conditions. These questions take the form of asking how much an individual is willing to pay or accept for some change in provision. Respondents are often reminded of the need to make compensating adjustments in other types of expenditure to accomodate this additional financial transaction.

Third, questions on socioeconomic and demographic characteristics of the respondent are asked in order to relate the answers that the respondents give to the valuation questions to the other characteristics of the respondent, and to those of the policy-relevant population.

2.6.1 Value elicitation
A respondent's choice or preference can be elicited in a number of ways. The simplest is to ask the respondent a direct question about how much he or she would be willing to pay for the good or service – known as continuous or open-ended questions. High rates of non–responses can be a problem with this approach. Alternatively, a respondent can be asked whether or not he or she would want to purchase the service if it cost a specified amount. These are known as discrete or dichotomous choice questions, and may be favoured because they do not give the respondent any incentive to answer untruthfully, that is the approach is 'incentive compatible'. A hybrid approach is the 'bidding game', where respondents are asked a series of questions to iterate towards a best estimate of their valuation. Alternatively, respondents may be shown a list of possible answers – a 'payment card' – and asked to indicate their choice, though this requires a careful determination of the range of possible answers. Each approach implies particular requirements in terms of statistical methods, and the appropriate choice for a specific problem is a matter of judgement on the part of the analyst.

2.6.2 Reliability of responses
If the variance in WTP responses to CV questions is large, the contingent valuation method could be described as unreliable in the sense that a researcher who attempted to elicit people's values would find it hard to know whether he or she would obtain the same answers if this approach to measurement were used

again. Variance in measurement of individuals' WTP could arise for a variety of reasons, including the sample size, the specificity of the CV scenario, and (for telephone and 'in person' interviews) the quality or performance of the enumerators on a given day. In order to test the reliability of the contingent valuation method, a few CV researchers have conducted tests of measurement replicability. These tests can be done in several ways. For example, respondents could be interviewed, and then at a later time reinterviewed and asked the same questions again. The few replicability tests that have been conducted to date have found a high correlation between the individuals' WTP in the test and retest experiments, indicating that the contingent valuation method appears to be a reliable measurement approach (Heberlein, 1986; Loehman and De, 1982; and Loomis, 1989, 1990).

2.6.3 Bias

Non-randomness in the variance of valuation responses can be caused by a number of factors which introduce bias into respondent behaviour. In this section we consider some of these biases, and the methods which can be employed to avoid or adjust to them.

The problem of strategic bias has long worried economists. The likelihood of the occurrence of strategic behaviour depends on the respondent's perceived payment obligation and his or her expectation about the provision of the good. Where individuals believe they will actually have to pay their reported WTP, but that their personal valuation will not affect whether the good is provided or not, there is a temptation to understate the true value in the hope of a 'free-ride', that is that others will pay. If, however, the price to be charged for the good is not tied to an individual's WTP response, whereas provision of the good is, then over-reporting of WTP might occur in order to ensure provision. Incentive compatible payment methods might minimise the risk of strategic behaviour. Overall, fears of strategic bias problems have not been substantiated by the large amount of empirical investigation into the question.

Hypothetical bias – caused by the hypothetical nature of the CV market – could mean that respondents' answers are meaningless if their declared intentions cannot be taken as an accurate guide to their actual behaviour. This is most likely to occur if respondents are very unfamiliar with the scenario presented to them. A careful and believable description of the good and its context can help in this instance. A survey of experimental tests, which compare hypothetical bids with those obtained in simulated markets where real money transactions take place, suggests that hypothetical bias can be reduced significantly if WTP formats are used instead of WTA, the reason being that respondents have more practical experience with payment than with compensation scenarios (Hanley, 1990).

Analysts will often wish to summarise respondents' valuation estimates in terms of the mean WTP for the good or service, or to develop an aggregate benefit estimate for a community or region. Two types of problems which might produce 'aggregation bias' involve sampling errors and insufficient sample sizes. Sampling errors might arise because survey non-responses are more likely to occur for certain types of individuals who are not randomly distributed in the population, resulting in a non-random survey sample. Similarly, if sample size is small, there is a risk that the characteristics of the sample will not be representative of the general population.

A number of studies have found evidence of 'payment vehicle bias', where WTP depends upon the choice of the method of payment, for instance, between tax increases or entrance fees. Controversial payment vehicles should be avoided in favour of those most likely to be employed in real life to elicit payment for the good in question. But the fact that the respondents' answers may depend on precisely how they are asked to pay for the hypothetical good or service should be expected; it should not be a source of concern because a preference for one payment vehicle over another may be perfectly reasonable. In this sense the term 'bias' is misplaced.

Starting point bias arises when the initial value suggested at the beginning of a bidding game has a significant impact upon the final bid reported by the respondent. The use of starting points can reduce valuation variance and the number of non-responses in open-ended type questionnaires, but at the possible expense of respondents not giving serious thought to their answers and taking cognitive 'short cuts' in arriving at their decision. One solution might be to use a 'payment card', with a range of numbers from which respondents can select their bid. However this can result in an 'anchoring' of bids within the range presented. It has been argued that an optimal range of prices should include a low price that results in almost all respondents accepting it, and a high price that results in almost all respondents rejecting it. Within this range, prices offered should reflect the distribution of bids so that, optimally, each bid interval reflects the same proportion of the population (see Bateman *et al.*, 1992).

Perhaps most controversy has centred on the so-called 'embedding effect'. A few studies have found that individuals' CV responses often do not vary significantly with changes in the scope and coverage of the environmental good being valued (Kahneman and Knetsch, 1992; Desvousges *et al.*, 1992). In these studies respondents appear not to discriminate between the particular environmental good under consideration, and the general class of environmental goods it belongs to. A number of explanations has been advanced for this phenomenon. Some have argued that it is because individuals' do not possess strongly articulated preferences for environmental goods, so that they tend to focus on other facets of the environment, such as the 'moral satisfaction' associated with the preservation of particular species or habitats (Kahneman and Knetsch, 1992) when deciding on a monetary valuation. Others have argued that embedding is more an artefact of poor survey design (for example Smith, 1992).

Another suggestion is that, to make valuation and financial decisions easier, people think in terms of a system of expenditure budgets, or 'mental accounts', to which they allocate their income (Thaler, 1984). If the amount allocated to the 'environment account' is quite small, then this might result in an inability to adjust valuations substantially in response to changes in the size and scope of an environmental good. Essentially, embedding might be a result of valuations' being determined by an income constraint which is inflexible and relatively strict compared with assessments of an individual's total (or full) income.

The debate over embedding has not yet been resolved. Whether the effect is a robust one or not, it does appear that its severity can be reduced by careful survey design, and in particular by giving precise, contextual descriptions of the good itself, and of the expenditure implications of a particular WTP bid.

2.6.4 Validity tests
A number of tests of the validity of contingent valuation studies exists (for example see Cummings *et al.*, 1986). 'Criterion validity' tests compare contingent valuations with 'true' values (the criterion) when these can be discerned in actual behaviour. Obviously, this is not feasible for many environmental goods, but experiments comparing hypothetical WTP sums with 'true' WTP as determined by simulated, 'real money' markets have found that, in general, WTP-format CVM studies can give valid estimates of true WTP.

'Construct validity' covers the results of CV studies in relation to both theoretical expectations ('theoretical validity') and the results of other valuation approaches ('convergent validity'). Tests of the former have centred on examining bid curve functions to see whether, for instance, elasticities have the correct sign and explanatory variables are significant. Tests of convergent validity are difficult because different approaches and studies often attempt to value different specifications of environmental goods. Furthermore, CV provides *ex ante* measures of WTP whilst other (indirect) approaches are *ex post* in nature. As such, the usefulness of convergent validity testing appears rather more limited than first anticipated.

2.6.5 Analysis of WTP responses
There are three ways in which CVM information is typically analysed to check the consistency of responses and to calculate the required valuation estimates.

Firstly, summary statistics such as means, medians and so on, can be used to calculate estimates of a good's total value for a particular population. Valuation frequency distributions can be used to estimate the proportion of a population that would be prepared to pay a given amount for the good.

Secondly, cross tabulations between WTP and socioeconomic and other variables are considered. When point estimates of WTP are available, mean WTP bids can be calculated for different groups of respondents, and then checked against the predictions of demand theory. Cross tabulations for dichotomous choice questions are also possible but require larger sample sizes to permit sufficiently powerful tests of differences between groups.

Thirdly, multivariate statistical techniques are used to estimate a valuation function that relates respondents' answers to hypothesised determinants of WTP, such as socioeconomic variables and the prices of substitute goods and services. Models can predict the actual amount that an individual with particular characteristics would be prepared to pay; the probability that he or she would value the good on offer at a given amount; or alternatively the proportion of the study population prepared to pay a given amount.

As an illustration of how contingent valuation responses are used to estimate respondents' WTP, consider the following example which uses discrete choice questions. Suppose a contingent valuation survey were conducted, and each respondent answered a single discrete choice question about whether they would vote for or against an environmental management plan, which would achieve a specified improvement in air quality in the urban area where they lived. Let's assume that the survey was designed so that there were five subsamples of respondents, each with about 20 percent of the total sample. Respondents have been randomly assigned to the five subsamples.

All the respondents in a given subsample were asked whether they would vote for or against the environmental management plan if it cost their household a specified price. The same price was given to all the respondents in a particular subsample, but different prices were presented to respondents in different subsamples. Suppose the results of the contingent valuation experiment were as follows:

1. Respondents in subsample 1 received a price of US$1 per month and 90 percent of them voted for the management plan and agreed to pay this price.
2. Respondents in subsample 2 received a price of $4 per month, and 75 percent of them agreed to vote for the management plan and pay this price.
3. Respondents in subsample 3 received a price of US$10 per month, and 50 percent of them indicated that they would vote for the plan and pay this price.
4. Respondents in subsample 4 received a price of US$20 per month and only 20 percent agreed to vote for the plan at this price.
5. Respondents in subsample 5 received a price of US$50 per month and only 5 percent said that they would vote for the plan at this price.

How can this information be used to calculate the average WTP of people in the city for the specified air quality improvement? If we can assume that the subsamples are large enough to be statistically representative of the overall population, then we can reason in the following manner. We know from the information obtained from subsample 1 that 10 percent of the population would not be willing to pay US$1 per month for the specified air quality improvement. Let's assume conservatively that this 10 percent of the population put zero value on the air quality improvement.

Comparing the results from subsamples 1 and 2, we see that 90 percent voted for the plan if it cost their household US$1 per month and only 75 percent if it cost US$4 per month. We thus conclude that 15 percent of the population places a value on the air quality improvement of between $1 (which these 15 percent would pay) and $4 (which they would not pay). Let's approximate the maximum WTP of this 15 percent of the population, and assume that on average the most they would be willing to pay would be $2.50 per month. Note that this group of 15 percent of the population that would be willing to pay a maximum of US$2.50 per month does not correspond to one of the five subsamples.

Similarly, consider subsamples 2 and 3. These results suggest that 25 percent of the population would be willing to pay $4 per month, but would not pay $10 per month. Let's approximate the maximum WTP of the average respondent in this group (25 percent of the population) as US$7 per month. Comparing subsamples 3 and 4, we see that 30 percent of the population would vote for the air quality improvement plan if it cost them $10 per month, but against the plan if it cost them $20 per month. We will assume the maximum WTP of the average respondent in this group is US$15 per month.

Next, we compare the results from subsamples 4 and 5 and find that 15 percent of the population would vote for the plan at US$20 per month but against the plan at US$50 per month. We again take the midpoint of this interval as an estimate of the maximum WTP of this group: US$35 per month. Finally, 5 percent of the population said they would vote for the management plan at the highest price offered – US$50 per month. What is the maximum WTP of this group? We do not know: let's conservatively put their value at US$50 per month (what they said they would pay). Thus we have the following results:

a) 10 percent of the population are not willing to pay anything for the specified air quality improvement;
b) 15 percent have a maximum value of US$2.50 per month on the air quality improvement;
c) 25 percent have a maximum value of US$7 per month;
d) 30 percent have a maximum value of US$15 per month;
e) 15 percent have a maximum value of US$35 per month; and
f) 5 percent have a maximum of US$50 per month.

With this information we can calculate the total WTP of the city. Assume the city has 300,000 households, and each respondent answers for one household. The total WTP per month for the management plan to improve air quality would be:

$$\text{Aggregate WTP} = (0.15)(300{,}000)(\text{US\$2.50}) + (0.25)(300{,}000)(\text{US\$7})$$
$$+ (0.30)(300{,}000)(\text{US\$15}) + (0.15)(300{,}000)(\text{US\$35})$$
$$+ (0.05)(300{,}000)(\text{US\$50})$$

(2.2)

$$= \$112{,}500 + \$525{,}000 + \$1{,}350{,}000$$
$$+ \$1{,}575{,}000 + \$750{,}000$$

$$= \$4{,}312{,}500 \text{ per month}$$

The average household WTP is thus:

$$\text{Average household WTP} = \$4{,}312{,}500 / 300{,}000 \text{ households}$$
$$= \$14.38 \text{ per month}$$

(2.3)

It should be emphasised that this approach of using discrete choice responses to a single valuation question to estimate WTP depends on an important assumption about the sample size. This assumption is that the sample is large enough so that it is reasonable to assume that if respondents in one subsample had been presented with a different price, they would have answered in the same way as the respondents in the subsample that did receive that price.

2.6.6 Conclusion on CVM

The US National Oceanic and Atmospheric Administration (NOAA) panel has offered a set of guidelines it believes should be followed if CV is to provide information about non-use values of sufficient quality as to be usable as the basis for claims for legal compensation for environmental damamge (Arrow *et al.*, 1994). The use of these guidelines within the profession is now being extended to cover all CV studies. CV is likely to be most reliable for valuing environmental gains, particularly when familiar goods are considered, such as local recreational amenities. Finally, it should be remembered that CVM is the only technique with the potential for measuring existence value.

2.7 Stated Preference Approaches – Contingent Ranking

Contingent ranking is implemented in the same vein as contingent valuation except that the respondent in the experiment is asked to rank order a large number of alternatives with various combinations of environmental goods and prices. A random utility framework (see section 2.6.2) is then used to analyse the data on the complete ranking of all the alternatives. The statistical estimation is often done with what is essentially a multinomial logit model of the rank order of the random utility level associated with each alternative. Implicit attribute prices or welfare change measures are then calculated from the parameter estimates of this logit model.

Applications of contingent ranking have usually involved the ranking of large numbers of alternatives, which often appear similar to the respondent. As such, the cognitive task of arriving at a complete ranking is found to be very difficult. Furthermore, the estimated statistical models are often poor and result in imprecise environmental values. The contingent ranking method has therefore met with a mixed response (Smith and Desvousges; 1986, Lareau and Rae, 1989).

2.8 Stated Preference Approaches – Conjoint Analysis

Conjoint analysis has strong foundations in psychology and statistics, but is rather shaky on theoretical foundation from the point of view of individual choice theory. However, there is a trend in valuation studies to move away from reliance on purely statistical methods towards more behaviourally based models such as multinomial logit model. One of the features of conjoint analysis is that each individual participating in the conjoint anlysis experiment is faced with a large number of ranking tasks. Each ranking task involves a small number of alternatives, for example, two. Then based on the collected data, some type of utility index model is estimated for one individual. This differs from contingent valuation and ranking where a large number of individuals are asked about their stated preferences for one set of alternatives, and a representative random utility model is estimated for the relevant population.

2.9 Indirect Valuation

Indirect valuation approaches seek to elicit environmental preferences from actual, observed, market-based information. In the surrogate market variant of indirect valuation, these markets are for private goods to which environmental commodities are related, either by being complements to or substitutes for the private goods in question. Individuals reveal their preferences for both the private and the environmental good when purchasing the private good, leaving what might be called a 'behavioral trail'. These techniques are therefore often preferred by policy makers because they rely on actual choices rather than the hypothetical choices involved in the direct valuation approaches. The other variant of indirect valuation, conventional market approaches, are used in situations where the output of an environmental good or service is measurable. These approaches use market prices (or shadow prices if markets are not efficient), or revealed/inferred prices (if no markets exist) to value some environmental impact.

2.10 Surrogate Market Approaches – Averting Behaviour

Perfect substitutability is the basis of the 'averting behaviour' technique, which looks at how averting inputs substitute for changes in environmental goods. For instance, expenditures on sound insulation can indicate householders' valuations of noise reduction; and expenditure on liming might reflect the benefits of reduced water acidification. The approach requires data on the environmental change and its associated substitution effects. Fairly crude approximations can be found simply by looking directly at the change in expenditure on the substitute good that arises as a result of some environmental change. Alternatively, the value per unit change of the environmental good can be determined. This is done by finding the marginal rate of substitution between the environmental commodity and the substitute private good from known or observed technical consumption data. The marginal rate of subsitiution is then multiplied by the price of the substitute private good, giving the value per unit change of the environmental good.

If the observed averting behaviour is not between two perfect substitutes, the benefits of the environmental good will be underestimated. For example, if there is an increase in environmental quality, the benefit of this change is given by the reduction in spending on the substitute market good required to keep the individual at their original level of welfare. However when the quality change takes place the individual will not reduce spending so as to stay at the original welfare level. Income effects will cause expenditure to be reallocated among all goods with a positive income elasticity of demand and so the reduction in spending on the substitute for environmental quality will not capture all of the benefits of the increase in quality.

Further problems with the approach include the fact that individuals may undertake more than one form of averting behaviour to any one environmental change, and that the averting behaviour may also have other beneficial effects which are not considered explicitly, for example sound insulation may also reduce heat loss from a home. Furthermore, averting behaviour is often not a continuous decision but a discrete one – a smoke alarm is either purchased or not, for instance. In this case the technique will again give an underestimate of benefits unless discrete choice models for averting behaviour are used.

Hence, simple avertive behaviour models can give incorrect estimates if they fail to incorporate the technical and behavioural alternatives to individuals' responses to quality changes. Nevertheless, although the technique has rarely been used, it is a potentially important source of valuation estimates since it gives theoretically correct estimates which are gained from actual expenditures and which thus have high criterion validity.

2.11 Surrogate Market Approaches – Travel Cost

Many natural resources, such as lakes and forests, are used extensively for the purpose of recreation. But it is often difficult to value these resources because no prices generally exist for them with which to estimate demand functions. However, travel cost models take advantage of the fact that, in most cases, a trip to a recreation site requires an individual to incur costs in terms of travel and time. Different individuals must incur different costs to visit different sites, and these 'implicit' prices can be used in place of conventional market prices as the basis for estimating the value of recreation sites and changes in their quality. Clearly, because travel cost models are concerned with active participation, they measure only the use value associated with any recreation site – option and existence values must be estimated via some other technique.

Two perspectives are possible. Simple travel cost models attempt to estimate the number of trips visited to a site or sites over some period of time, perhaps a season. 'Random utility models' consider the specific decision of whether to visit a recreation site, and if so, which one. We will briefly deal with each in turn.

2.11.1 The simple travel cost model
There are two variants of the simple travel cost visitation model. The first can be used to estimate (representative) individuals' recreation demand functions. This is done by observing the visitation rate of individuals who make trips to a recreational facility, as a function of the travel cost. The value of a recreation site to an individual is measured by the area under his or her demand curve, so that the total recreation (use) value of a site is simply the area under each demand curve summed over all individuals. This 'individual' travel cost model requires that there is variation in the number of trips individuals make to the recreational site, in order to estimate the demand function. One particular problem therefore arises from the fact that such variation is not always observed, especially since all individuals do not always make a positive number of trips to a recreational site. Some individuals do not make any. This means that if we are to use standard statistical techniques such as Ordinary Least Squares (OLS) for the analysis of such models, we must exclude non-participants from our data sample. This will not only imply probably very low participation rates, but also a loss of potentially useful information about the participation decision. However including all individuals in a sampling area does mean that more complex statistical methods are required – in particular, discrete choice models.

Alternatively, a simpler solution is to model the demand for a site as an aggregate or market demand, using the standard statistical techniques. This second variant of simple travel cost models is known as the 'zonal' travel cost method. The unit of observation is now the 'zone', as opposed to the individual. The visitation rate used is the number of trips per capita from each zone. Zones are constructed by dividing the region around a site into areas of increasing travel cost. The observations of trips are then allocated to their 'zone of origin', and the population of each zone is found. The visitation rate is calculated by dividing the number of trips from each zone by the population in the zone.

In general, individual travel cost models are preferred to the zonal variant. This is because the zonal model is statistically inefficient, since it aggregates data from a large number of individual observations into a few zonal observations. In addition, the zonal model treats all individuals from within a zone as having the same travel costs, when this is often clearly not the case (especially with respect to opportunity costs of travel time – see Section 2.11.2).

For both variants of the simple model, the demand curves are estimated by regressing visitation rates on socioeconomic characteristics (for example income), estimates of the costs of visiting a site, and some indicator of site quality.

The simple travel cost models are estimated with data collected from surveys of either visitors to a recreational site, or households in a general population. In either case, the data requirements of this approach are potentially significant, since data are required on each individual's own characteristics (or population characteristics), as well as on the nature of their trip, the distance and time travelled, the costs of travel, and so on. These data are generally gained from some existing or specially commissioned survey. Site quality is often a somewhat intangible variable. Simple measures may concentrate on indicators such as angling catch rates, while others may be based on, for instance, biochemical indicators such as dissolved oxygen. The issue here, of course, is whether the measures selected coincide in any robust way with those which individuals perceive to be relevant.

Unless the recreational site being valued is unique, most individuals will have access to a range of substitute sites that they could use for the same or similar recreational activity. Omitting these substitute sites will lead to bias in our benefit estimates, although there is no simple way of incorporating substitutes into this version of the model. Including all possible substitutes is obviously impractical, so judgement is needed on the part of the researcher. Multi-site models vary in their complexity and their ability to explain substitution behaviour. Often, restrictions are placed on site characteristics (for example models refer to some 'typical' site) or demand equations (for example 'pooled' models). Morey's (1984, 1985) 'share' model considers the allocation of an individual's fixed time budget between sites, thus being able to account for site substitution at the expense of being unable to explain the total amount of time allocated to recreation.

2.11.2 Time costs

Since the costs of visiting a site consist of the transportation costs plus the costs of the time spent at and getting to the site, the role of time is critical to the estimation of travel costs. We need to know what elements of time are to be included in the travel costs, and what money values to use for these time costs. Clearly, time needs to be accounted for because it is a scarce resource, and time spent in one activity could be spent on another, that is time has an opportunity cost. If we ignore it, estimated benefits of recreation will be biased, downwards in the case of travel time, upwards in the case of on-site time.

The (marginal) wage rate is often used as an approximate shadow price of time, since this reflects the opportunity cost of time between working and not working. However, this trade-off may be distorted by institutional constraints such as maximum working hours, taxation, and so on. Further, using the wage rate may be inappropriate for certain groups such as the retired or unemployed. Previous empirical work has suggested that the shadow price of time may be substantially less than the wage rate. Some studies determine the proportion of the wage rate to use within the estimation procedure, for example Common (1973), McConnell and Strand (1981).

2.11.3 Measuring welfare changes

Some environmental changes can cause sites to become suitable or unsuitable for any particular recreational activity. For instance, acid deposition can cause the acidification of surface waters, killing fish populations and effectivly deleting that site as a possibility for fishing. The value of a particular site is equal to the area under the demand curve for that site, taking substitutes and so on into account, measured between the current price for site access – given by the relevant travel cost – and the price at which individuals would choose not to visit at all. This latter can be derived from the estimated recreation demand function. Technically, we integrate the estimated demand function between these two prices.

Recreation sites can also change in quality. For the fishing example above, acidification might reduce catch rates, or change the type of fish present. Such changes are likely to cause a shift in the relevant recreation demand curve. Variations in quality across sites can be accounted for by the various types of multi-site models mentioned above, with quality included simply as another variable. Sometimes a 'price–quality interaction' term is used, as in the 'varying parameter' model, see Vaughan and Russell, 1982; Smith and Desvousges, 1985. The shift in the demand function is then simulated by inserting the new vector of quality attributes into the estimated function. The value of the change is given by the difference between the areas under these two demand curves, estimated as before.

We should be careful to account for the possible impact of income effects when we are valuing price and/or quality changes. Evidence suggests that they are not likely to be large for relatively common recreation sites (Freeman, 1993). Some estimate of the likely bias induced by income effects can be obtained when quality is not a significant factor. However when quality does vary considerably, no simple approach is available (see Bockstael, McConnell and Strand, 1991).

As an example of the simple zonal travel cost model, Table 2.3 describes data which can be used to estimate a demand curve for recreational fishing at a specific site. The demand curve is used to estimate the total value of the consumers' surplus obtained from the site. Column 1 of the table lists the 4 cities (zones) from which visitors visit the site. The cities are labelled A, B, C, D. The second column lists the population of each of the cities. The third column lists the number of visits per year from each city, and the fourth column lists the costs of travelling to the site from each city. If we divide the number of visits per year from each city by the population of each city then we get the visitation rates shown in column 5 for each city.

We now postulate that a linear relationship can be used to predict visitation rate (the number of visits per capita) from each city in terms of the travel cost from that city. Such a relationship is described by the equation:

$$V_z/Pop_z = a - b.TC_z \tag{2.4}$$

Now using regression analysis (Ordinary Least Squares) we can estimate this equation for the data given in Table 2.3. This gives the following estimated equation:

$$V_z/Pop_z = 0.5 - 0.1\ TC_z \tag{2.5}$$

Using this equation we can calculate the predicted number of visits per capita from each city to the site as shown in column 3 of Table 2.4, and use this to draw a graph with travel cost (price) per visit on the vertical axis and predicted per capita visits to the site on the horizontal axis (Figure 2.1). This is the estimated demand curve, and we can now use this to calculate the consumers' surplus obtained by a representative visitor in each of the 4 cities. Consumers surplus is given by the area between the demand curve and the price paid (travel cost).

For example the per capita consumers' surplus for a visitor from city D is given by the area of region 1 in Figure 2.1 (since travel cost is $4). Likewise the per capita consumers' surplus obtained by a visitor from city C is given by the combined area of regions 1 and 2 (since travel cost is $3); for city B it is the combined area of regions 1, 2 and 3 (travel cost is $2); and for city A it is the combined area of regions 1, 2, 3 and 4 (travel cost is $1).

Table 2.3 Trips to a recreational fishing site from four cities

City	Population	Total Visits per year	Travel Cost per visit	Visitation Rate
	(Pop)	(V)	(TC)	(V/Pop)
A	1000	450	$1	0.45
B	2000	600	$2	0.15
C	3000	700	$3	0.35
D	4000	200	$4	0.05

Table 2.4 Valuation of trips to a recreational fishing site from four cities

City	Travel Cost per visit	Predicted Annual Visits per capita	Per Capita Consumers' Surplus	Total Consumers' Surplus
A	$1	0.40	0.80	800
B	$2	0.30	0.45	1800
C	$3	0.20	0.20	400
D	$4	0.10	0.05	200

Per capita consumers' surplus is shown in column 4 of Table 2.4, and if we multiply each by the population in each respective city we obtain an estimate of the total annual consumers' surplus in each city generated by the site, as shown in column 5 of Table 2.4. The total annual consumers' surplus produced by the site for consumers for all 4 cities is 3,200 dollars.

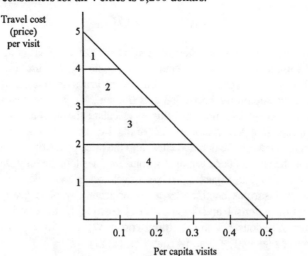

Figure 2.1 Predicted per capita visits and travel cost per visit

2.11.4 Random Utility Models

The Random Utility Model (RUM) considers the decision about which recreation site to visit for any one choice occasion. Hence, it is particularly suitable for cases where the major component of recreation behaviour is substitution between sites, as is the case with water-based recreation sites (Bockstael, McConnell and Strand, 1991). Unfortunately, RUMs cannot readily predict the total amount of recreation that will occur. This implies that if, as a result of some environmental change, more people decide to participate more often, the benefits of this extra activity will not be captured by the RUM.

The probability that a particular individual will visit a specific recreation site is equal to the probability that the utility derived from a visit to that site is greater than the utility that would be derived from a visit to any other site. If we make various assumptions, this probability can be obtained by estimating an indirect utility function using maximum likelihood methods. The change in welfare from a change in quality is obtained by estimating the function first with the 'before' and then with the 'after' vector of quality characteristics. The value of the change is given by the difference in the values of these two estimations. Freeman (1993) presents a thorough discussion of the approach.

The difficulty with predicting the total amount of recreation activity can be addressed in a number of ways. One approach is to extend the range of activity options available to include non-participation. To avoid bias in the regression coefficients, the participation decision is best treated separately as an initial choice problem. Unfortunately, the data are rarely available to explain participation well. This is also a problem which is faced by participation models.

2.11.5 Participation models

We mention participation models briefly here primarily because of their relevance to the benefits transfer discussion in Section 2.10. These have the advantage of involving less stringent assumptions and estimation techniques. A two-stage approach is generally followed (for example Vaughan and Russell, 1982) – a logit model to predict whether an individual participates or not, and a second equation to predict the amount of recreation 'consumed' given that an individual is a participant. This second equation usually includes a range of socioeconomic variables, and some measures of the availability and quality of recreational resources. Changes in participation can be estimated by inputing alternative values for the quantity and quality variables.

These changes are often valued in the following way. Travel cost or contingent valuation studies of recreation are used to derive values for a 'recreation day'. These can be obtained directly from contingent valuation studies; for travel cost, the estimated value of the site is divided by the number of activity days or visits. Then the per day value is multiplied by the estimated change in the number of days to give a total value of the environmental change. Clearly, then, average values are used when marginal values are strictly appropriate. Moreover, no account can be taken of the possibility that environmental changes might increase the value of a recreation day.

Perhaps most worryingly, as Vaughan and Russell (1982) and Morey (1992) have demonstrated, the margin of error between the exact welfare change and that estimated by this 'participation approach' can be significant. The error is greatest when we are dealing with non-marginal changes in participation, such as happens when a recreation site is eliminated or created, as with our example of water acidification and fisheries.

2.11.6 Conclusions on travel cost

The general travel cost method is a technically well-developed valuation approach which has been extensively employed over the past two decades. It is useful because it is grounded, at least in theory, on actual observed behaviour. However, the technical and data requirements should not be underestimated; travel cost is unlikely to be a low cost approach to non-market valuation.

2.12 Surrogate Market Approaches – Hedonic Pricing

Like avertive behaviour and travel cost, hedonic pricing also requires the weak complementarity assumption. However, it differs in that it operates through changes in the prices rather than quantities of private goods. A private good to which environmental quality is complementary can be viewed as a bundle of characteristics which includes environmental quality. Then, individuals express their preferences for environmental quality by their selection of a particular bundle of characteristics. These preferences will be reflected in the differential prices paid for private goods in the market. The hedonic pricing approach applies econometric techniques to data on private good characteristics and prices to derive estimates of the implicit prices for environmental quality.

For instance, the location of residential property can affect the environmental attributes of that property, and potentially, therefore, the stream of benefits associated with residence. Let us assume that the expected stream of these benefits is capitalised in property values. Then the value of two properties which differ only in, say, the local air quality, will differ to the extent that people find one level of air quality preferable to the other. The difference in value can be viewed as the implicit price of the difference in air quality. Even when properties differ in many ways, not just in environmental quality, we might still be able to uncover the implicit prices if our data and statistical techniques are good enough.

2.12.1 The hedonic price function

The first stage of the hedonic price approach is to specify and estimate an hedonic price function, which relates house prices to all the relevant characteristics of the housing stock. More formally, it describes all points of equilibrium between sellers' offers of different environmental quality at different prices, and buyers' bids for environmental quality at those prices.

The marginal implicit price of each characteristic is given by the respective partial differential of the hedonic price function, that is the responsiveness of property price to a change in the characteristic in question. This price does not have to be constant, and indeed, we might expect the implicit price of a characteristic to fall as the quantity supplied increases. The price of one characteristic might also depend on the level of a different characteristic. However, rather than imposing any restrictions on the analysis, it is customary to see what functional form of the hedonic price function (and hence the form of the marginal implicit price function) fits the data best.

The preferred data include the sale prices associated with actual property market transactions; housing characteristics (for example number of rooms, type of neighbourhood); and environmental characteristics (for example noise, air quality). This presumed superiority of characteristics over, say, individuals' own valuations of their property does imply some stringent assumptions – in particular, that the housing market is in equilibrium. Violation of this assumption could result in a benefit estimate which is either an upper or lower bound on the true benefit, although we should be able to tell which is the case in any particular study. Moreover, there is the obvious problem of how to measure qualitative variables such as air pollution in objective terms. Here, we encounter again the usual question of whether individuals' perceptions of qualitative variables can be related to objective, or policy-relevant measures. Similarly, can the changes in individual environmental variables be discerned, or must we work in terms of some 'overall' environmental quality? Furthermore, when variables are correlated, we face the uncertain trade-off of bias being introduced due to significant explanatory variables being omitted to reduce problems of multicollinearity.

2.12.2 The bid function
We cannot generally use the estimated hedonic price function directly to value changes in environmental quality. This is because this function is a locus of supply and demand equilibria, whereas it is the demand (or bid) function alone which is relevant for benefit estimation. The hedonic price function will trace out the desired bid function only when all individuals are identical in tastes and preferences. However, even if all individuals are identical, the bid function cannot be identified if all individuals face the same implicit price for the environmental attribute to be valued. But this implicit price does at least reflect the marginal WTP of each individual for improved quality, and so could be used to value marginal changes in environmental quality. Unfortunately, environmental changes of most policy interest are often not marginal.

Hence, the second stage of the hedonic pricing approach generally involves regressing our implicit price estimates from the hedonic price function on physical and socio-economic variables thought to influence housing demand. If we assume that the supply of housing is fixed in the short run, this should allow us to identify the bid function we seek. However, the problem of identification should not be underestimated. All consumers within a housing market face the same equilibrium price schedule, or hedonic price function. Hence, the observation of a single consumer's behaviour provides only one point on that consumer's bid function. Other marginal prices are observed only for other individuals, so they provide no indication of the likely reaction of the original consumer to varying prices.

A number of solutions to the identification problem have been proposed. One option is to restrict variables or functional forms to be different in the second stage from those employed in the first stage, although this restriction cannot always be justified. The preferred alternative is to use data from spatially or temporally-separated markets, so that individuals do not face the same hedonic price function. This does, however, require that consumers are similar between these separate markets.

2.12.3 Measuring welfare changes

We will only be able to use the hedonic price function to measure welfare changes when the accompanying environmental change is marginal, or if we assume either that all individuals are identical, or that the number of houses affected is small. Otherwise, welfare measurement will most likely be via the estimated bid functions. Unfortunately, obtaining an exact estimate of the change in welfare is not an easy task.

However, we can get a lower bound estimate of the welfare change if we assume that individuals do not move house in response to the change in environmental quality. This might not be unrealistic – given the presence of moving costs, and of other factors which affect the decision to move, we might expect environmental quality to affect the choice of house only after the prior decision to move has been taken. This being the case, an estimate of the benefits of increased environmental quality is given by the integral of the estimated bid function between the two levels of environmental quality considered.

2.12.4 Other issues

The property value variant of the hedonic approach we have considered here can be extended in a number of ways. For instance, the effects of property and income taxation need to be accounted for if capital asset prices are to be translated into annual benefit streams. If individuals are able to take avertive action in response to, say, air pollution, the marginal implicit price for air quality improvements (derived from the hedonic price function) will reflect the cost of these averting activities. If averting behaviour affects the characteristics of a particular house (for instance, if air filters are installed), this may need to be accounted for in the specification of the hedonic price function.

The hedonic approach relies on the assumptions of a freely functioning and efficient property market. Individuals have perfect information and mobility so that they can buy the exact property and associated characteristics that they desire and so reveal their demand for environmental quality. In reality the housing market is unlikely to be thus. A large part of the housing stock may be in the public sector and so allocated subject to price controls. Furthermore market segmentation may exist so that mobility between housing areas is restricted. Nevertheless, the hedonic approach is founded upon a sound theoretical base and is capable of producing valid estimates of benefits so long as individuals can perceive environmental changes. It has been employed to produce reliable estimates of the value of actual environmental changes.

2.12.5 Hedonic wages

The hedonic pricing approach has been applied to factors of production as well as to consumption goods. Labour is an obvious example, where we look at the supply of and demand for a set of job characteristics or attributes that together define the job in question. The wage rate is the overall 'price' of the job, but this price is made up of a set of hedonic prices relating to each characteristic, such as tasks involved, working conditions, accident risks and so on.

If the labour market functions freely then the mixture of job characteristics will adjust to clear markets for each type of labour. Other things being equal, jobs with a higher risk of accidents will be expected to pay a higher wage than otherwise. Furthermore, if firms incur expenditures in reducing the risks of accidents then it is expected that they will want to pay lower wages than otherwise. We therefore have the potential for beneficial trade between the two so that a price of safety is obtained.

Just as was described above for hedonic pricing for property characteristics, the wage risk approach identifies any systematic differences in the wage rates of jobs and tries to separate out the influence of safety on the wages. We can then identify what part of any wage differential is due to differences in the safety risks of the job, and from this infer what the benefits are of improving safety.

2.13 Conventional Market Approaches – Dose–Response

The dose–response technique aims to establish a relationship between environmental impacts (the response) and some cause of the impact such as pollution (the dose). When the impact shows up in changes in the quantity or price of marketed inputs or outputs, the value of the change can be measured by changes in the total of 'consumer plus producer surplus'.

The technique is used extensively where dose–response relationships between some cause of damage such as pollution, and output/impacts are known. For example, it has been used to look at the effect of pollution on health, physical effects on materials and buildings, aquatic ecosystems, vegetation and soil erosion. The physical dose–response function is multiplied by a unit 'price' or value per unit of physical damage to give a 'monetary damage function'.

When the response to a 'dose' of pollution is marginal, we might be able to value the impact directly at current market prices. However, when output responses are not marginal, a more general approach is warranted. For instance, even if all prices remain unchanged, producers might change the quantity of other inputs into their production processes, implying different costs and a change in producer surplus. If the output price does change, consumers' consumption patterns will change, as will their consumer surplus. Hence, non-marginal output responses are likely to require a modelling approach to predict changes in prices and behaviour on both the supply and demand side of the relevant markets. The effects of government intervention and market imperfection may also have to be incorporated (for example through shadow pricing).

Such prediction of market responses is complicated. Individuals will often make complex changes in their behaviour to protect themselves against any effects (averting behaviour). Farmers might switch to crop varieties which are resistant to air pollution. Materials corrosion might be countered by painting, switching to corrosion-resistant substitutes, or simply replacing the materials more often. A large number of markets might be involved, and modelling such an interrelated system can be an extremely sophisticated or fairly simple activity. The simpler models can provide useful estimates provided their shortcomings are recognized.

The specification of the dose–response relationship is crucial to the accuracy of the approach. The pollutant responsible for the damage needs to be identified as well as all possible variables affected. Large quantities of data may thus be required. Often there may be subtle but potentially significant forms of damage that are easy to observe and measure, for example leaf-drop and discolouring in vegetation. These can be used as variables in the dose–response function. However, some effects such as reduced plant vigour and less resilience to pests may be difficult to observe and measure directly. In such cases it is necessary to use an 'instrumental variable' in the dose–response function, that is one that is easily measurable and which indicates the level of damage, even if that damage cannot be measured directly. In some cases, the damage might not be economically relevant if individuals are not concerned by it. For instance, leaf loss and discoloration may have no impact upon the amenity or commercial value of forests.

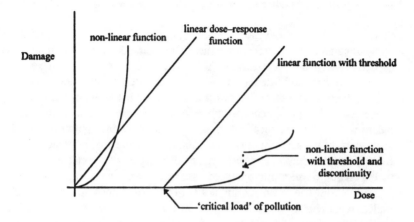

Figure 2.2 Damage thresholds

There is a further difficulty with isolating the effects of one cause from that of others in determining the impact on a receptor (for example synergistic effects where several pollutants or sources exist), and also with isolating other factors such as climate which may vary by area. Positive ambient levels of pollution might occur naturally, so that attributing all damage to man-made sources may overstate the situation. Identification of damage threshold levels may be important in the specification of the dose–response relationship as shown in Figure 2.2. The long term effects of low to medium levels of pollution may be unidentifiable, especially in the case of ecosystem behaviour. Discontinuities in the dose–response function may also exist. All these problems result in difficulty in the empirical specification of the functional form.

To conclude, the dose–response approach is a technique that can be used in cases where the physical and ecological relationships between pollution and output or impact are known. The approach cannot estimate non-use values. The approach is theoretically sound, with any uncertainty residing mainly in specifying the dose–response relationships themselves, and in predicting behavioural responses to impacts. The approach may be costly to undertake if large databases need to be manipulated for physical and economic modelling. However if the dose–response functions already exist and impacts are marginal, the method can be very inexpensive, with low time demands, providing reasonable first approximations of the true economic value measures. In the case of air pollution damage, the dose–response function is in fact the main technique used to derive economic values.

2.14 Conventional Market Approaches – Replacement Cost

This technique looks at the cost of replacing or restoring a damaged asset to its original state and uses this cost as a measure of the benefit of restoration. The approach is widely used because it is often easy to find estimates of such costs.

The approach is valid when it is possible to argue that the remedial work must take place because of some other constraint such as an environmental standard. Replacement will only be economically efficient, however, if the environmental standard was itself economically determined. Otherwise, the approach estimates only the costs of replacement: it is not a technique for benefit estimation.

Information on replacement costs can be obtained from direct observation of actual spending on restoring damaged assets or from engineering estimates of restoration costs. The technique implies various assumptions, for instance, that complete replacement is, in fact, feasible. In general, because of the highlighted potential for confusion between costs and benefits, the replacement cost technique should be used with some care.

2.15 Benefits Transfer

It is not always necessary to initiate a new study in a project area to determine how the wellbeing of individuals might be affected by some environmental change. If a similar project has previously been undertaken elsewhere, estimates of its economic consequences might be usable as an indicator of the impacts of the new project.

Suppose we wished to estimate the water-based benefits of controlling acid rain in the UK. Rather than implementing a completely new study, we might be able to identify previous studies that have considered this issue, and then assume that these prior estimates of benefits are indicative of the benefits that we might expect in the UK. Such an approach has been termed 'benefits transfer' because the estimates of economic benefits are 'transferred' from a site where a study has already been completed to a site of policy interest. The benefits transferred from the study site could have been measured using any of the direct or indirect valuation techniques outlined above. There are three broad approaches to benefits transfer to consider here.

2.15.1 Transferring average benefit estimates
Here we assume that the change in wellbeing experienced on average by individuals at existing sites is equal to that which will be experienced at the new site. Previous studies are used to estimate the consumer surplus or average WTP of individuals engaged in, say, recreational activities of various kinds. The value of a 'person-day' for each recreational activity at existing sites is multiplied by the forecast change in the number of days at the new site, to obtain estimates of

the aggregate economic benefits of recreation at the new site (see the discussion of 'participation models' in section 2.6.2 above).

For a variety of reasons, individuals at the new site may not value its recreational possibilities the same as individuals at the existing sites on which the unit values are based. Moreover, average benefit estimates might ignore the value of environmental changes to existing users of a recreation site. Perhaps most worryingly, as Vaughan and Russell (1982) and Morey (1992) demonstrate, the margin of error in estimating the true change in recreational value can be considerable with this method, especially when the environmental change we are considering is discrete, for example the creation or elimination of recreation sites.

2.15.2 Transferring adjusted average benefit values
Here the mean unit values of the existing studies are adjusted before transferral to the new site, in order to account for any biases that are thought to exist, or to reflect better the conditions at the new site. These differences might be in socioeconomic characteristics of households, in the environmental change being looked at, and in the availability of substitute goods and services. Clearly, however, the adjusted approach is still subject to many of the qualifications noted in the previous section.

2.15.3 Transferring benefit functions
Instead of transferring adjusted or unadjusted average values, the entire demand function estimated at existing sites could be transferred to the new site. More information is passed over in this way. As an example (Loomis, 1992), for a zonal travel cost model, the demand function might be of the form:

$$X_{ij}/POP_i = b_0 - b_1 C_{ij} + b_2 TIME_{ij} + b_3 P^s_{ik} + b_4 I_i + b_5 Q_j \qquad (2.6)$$

where X_{ij} is the number of trips from origin zone i to site j; POP_i is the population of origin zone i; C_{ij} is travel costs from origin zone i to site j; P^s_{ik} is a measure of the cost and quality of substitute site k for people in origin zone i; I_i is average income of people in origin zone i; and Q_j is the quality of site j for recreational uses.

Estimates of the parameters b_n are needed from existing studies. Policy–site data are then collected on the variables in the transferred function. This new equation is then used to estimate both the number of trips to the new site and the average household WTP for a visit to the new site.

Benefits transfer is still in its infancy, in part because for many environmental policy issues only a limited number of high quality valuation studies have been completed. However, it is potentially a very important and useful estimation approach, as it could feasibly provide accurate and robust benefit estimates at a fraction of the cost of a full-blown valuation study.

REFERENCES

Arrow, K., Solow, R., Schuman, H., Ragner, R. and Portney, P. (1994), 'Report to the NOAA Panel on Contingent Valuation', *US Federal Register*, **58** (10) 4602–4614.

Bateman, I.J., Willis, K.G., Garrod, G.D., Doktor, P., Langford, I. and Turner, R.K. (1992), *Recreation and Environmental Preservation Value of the Norfolk Broads: A Contingent Valuation Study*, Report to the National Rivers Authority, Environmental Appraisal Group, University of East Anglia, pp. 403.

Bockstael, N., McConnell, K. and Strand, I. (1991), 'Recreation', in Braden, J.B. and Kolstad, C.D. (eds), *Measuring the Demand for Environmental Quality*, Amsterdam: North Holland.

Cichetti, C., Fisher, A. and Smith, V.K. (1971), 'An Econometric Evaluation of a Generalized Consumer Surplus Measure: The Mineral King Controversy', *Econometrica*, **39**, 813–827.

Common, M.S. (1973), 'A Note on the Use of the Clawson Method for the Evaluation of Recreational Sight Benefits', *Regional Studies*, **7**, 401–406.

Cummings, R.G., Brookshire, D.S. and Schulze, W.D. (1986), *Valuing Environmental Goods: An Assessment of the Contingent Valuation Method*, Totowa, NJ: Rowman & Allanheld.

Desvousges, W.H., Johnson, F.R., Dunford, R.W., Boyle, K.J., Hudson, S.P. and Wilson, K.N. (1992), *Measuring Nonuse Damages Using Contingent Valuation: An Experimental Evaluation of Accuracy*, Research Triangle Institute Monograph 92-1, Research Triangle Park, NC: Research Triangle Institute.

Dubourg, W.R., Loomes, G. and Jones-Lee, M.W. (1994), 'Imprecise Preferences and the WTP–WTA Disparity', *Journal of Risk and Uncertainty*, **9**, (2).

Freeman, A.M. III (1993), *The Measurement of Environmental and Resource Values – Theory and Methods*, Washington DC: Resources for the Future.

Hanemann, W.M. (1991), 'Willingness-to-Pay versus Willingness-to-Accept: How Much Can They Differ?', *American Economic Review*.

Hanley, N.D. (1990), *'Valuation of Environmental Effects: Final Report – Stage One'*, Industry Department of Scotland and the Scottish Development Agency.

Heberlein, T.A. (1986), *'Measuring Resource Values: The Reliability and Validity of Dichotomous Contingent Valuation Measures'*, Paper presented at the American Sociological Association Meeting, New York.

Hicks J.R. (1939), 'The Foundations of Welfare Economics', *Economic Journal*, **49** (196), 696–712.

Kahneman, D. and Knetsch, J. (1992), 'Valuing Public Goods: The Purchase of Moral Satisfaction', *Journal of Environmental Economics and Management*, **22** (1) 57–70.

Kahneman, D. and Tversky, A. (1979), 'Prospect Theory: An Analysis of Decision under Risk', *Econometrica*, **XLVII**, 263–291.

Kahneman, D., Knetsch, J. and Thaler, R. (1990), 'Experimental Tests of the Endowment Effect and the Coase Theorem', *Journal of Political Economy*, **98**, 1325–48.

Kaldor, N. (1939), 'Welfare Propositions of Economics and Interpersonal Comparisons of Utility', *Economic Journal*, 49, 549–552.

Knetsch, J.L. (1990), 'Environmental Policy Implications of Disparities between Willingness to Pay and Compensation Demanded Measures of Values', *Journal of Environmental Economics and Management*, 18 (3), 227–237.

Lareau, T.J. and Rae, D.A. (1989), 'Valuing WTP for Diesel Odor Reductions: An Application of Contingent Ranking Technique', *Southern Economic Journal*, 55 (3), 728–742.

Loehman, E.T. and De, V.H. (1982), 'Application of Stochastic Choice Modelling to Policy Analysis of Public Goods: A Case Study of Air Quality Improvements', *Review of Economics and Statistics*, 64, 474–480.

Loomis, J.B. (1989), 'Test–Retest Reliability of the Contingent Valuation Method: A Comparison of General Population and Visitor Response', *American Journal of Agricultural Economics*, 71, 76–84.

Loomis, J.B. (1990), 'Comparative Reliability of the Dichotomous Choice and Open Ended Valuation Techniques', *Journal of Environmental Economics and Management*, 18 (1), 78–85.

Loomis, J.B. (1992), 'The Evolution of a More Rigorous Approach to Benefit Transfer: Benefit Transfer Function', *Water Resources Research*, 28 (3), (Special Section: Problems and Issues in the Validity of Benefit Transfer Methodologies).

McConnell, K.E. and Strand, I.E. (1981), 'Measuring the Cost of Time in Recreation Demand Analysis', *American Journal of Agricultural Economics*, 63, 153–156.

Morey, E.R. (1984), 'The Choice of Ski Areas: Estimation of a Generalised CES Preference Ordering with Characteristics', *Review of Economics and Statistics*, 66, 584–590.

Morey, E.R. (1985), 'Characteristics, Consumer Surplus, and New Activities: A Proposed Ski Area', *Journal of Public Economics*, 26 (2), 221–236.

Morey, E.R. (1992), *What is consumer's surplus per day of use? And what does it tell us about consumer's surplus?*, AERE Workshop on Benefits Transfer, Snowbird, Utah.

Pearce, D.W., Moran, D. and Fripp, E. (1992), *The Economic Value of Biological and Cultural Diversity*, A Report to the World Conservation Union, Centre for Social and Economic Research on the Global Environment.

Smith, V.K. (1992), 'Arbitrary Values, Good Causes, and Premature Verdicts', *Journal of Environmental and Resource Economics*, 22 (1), 71–89.

Smith, V.K. and Desvousges, W.H. (1986), *Measuring Water Quality Benefits*, Boston: Kluwer–Nijhoff Publishing.

Thaler, R. (1984), 'Towards a Positive Theory of Consumer Choice', *Journal of Economic Behaviour and Organisation*, 1 (1), 29–60.

Tversky, A. and Kahneman, D. (1981), 'The Framing of Decisions and the Psychology of Choice', *Science*, 211, 453–458.

Vaughan, W.J. and Russell, C.S. (1982), 'Valuing a Fishing Day: An Application of a Systematic Varying Parameter Model', *Land Economics*, 58 (4), 451–463.

Willig, R.D. (1976), 'Consumers' Surplus Without Apology', *American Economic Review*, 66 (4), 589–597.

3. Selected Case Studies in Economic Valuation

3.1 Introduction

This chapter takes a closer look at some selected case studies in an effort to illustrate the kinds of procedures available to derive economic values. The studies illustrate the different methodologies and the various problems of applying those methodologies in the developing world.

3.2 Contingent Valuation: Household Demand for Improved Sanitation in Kumasi, Ghana.

Whittington, D., Lauria D.T., Wright A., Choe K., Hughes J., and Swarna V. (1993), 'Household Demand for Improved Sanitation Services in Kumasi, Ghana: A Contingent Valuation Study', *Water Resources Research*, **29** (6), pp. 1,539–1,560.

3.2.1 Introduction

In most cities in industrialised countries, households do not have a choice about whether or not to connect the sanitary facilities in their house to a sewer. Every household may be required by law to connect if access is provided. This regulatory approach can only work, however, when the vast majority of households clearly have sufficient financial resources to pay for the sewerage system and the connection. In many developing countries, this is not the case: issues of affordability and households' WTP for improved sanitation services are often much less clear. If households in a city of a developing country are required by law to connect to a sewerage system but the costs of the system including connections are much higher than the majority of households are able and willing to pay, then subsidies from some level of government will be required to cover the deficit. If subsidies are not available, such a regulation typically cannot be enforced.

This situation is now commonplace in many cities in developing countries. Many sewerage systems have been built that people cannot afford to connect to and are thus not being used. Households are often unwilling to pay for even the operation and maintenance of sewerage systems. Because large subsidies for the construction of sewerage systems are increasingly difficult to obtain, user charges in the form of sewer connection fees and monthly tariffs must be relied upon to an increasing extent to finance sanitation improvements. However, the process of establishing a tariff structure requires detailed information on how specific groups of households will respond to various combinations of monthly tariffs and connection fees. Such information on household demand for improved sanitation services is rarely available: it must be collected by the government agencies and donors involved before sanitation planning in developing countries can be improved. This study used the contingent valuation method to gather such information.

3.2.2 Fieldwork and data collection

The field work for this research was carried out over a five-month period from July to November, 1989. An initial version of the household questionnaire was developed over a three-week period of intensive experimentation in July, 1989. Approximately 50 household interviews and open-ended, small group discussions were conducted with respondents throughout Kumasi. The household questionnaire was then pretested with 100 households.

The final survey questionnaire had four parts. The first consisted of several questions about demographic characteristics of the respondent and his or her household (such as the number of family members and whether the respondent was head of the household). The second part included questions about the household's existing water and sanitation situation: type of facilities used, monthly expenditures, and household satisfaction with its existing sanitation facility, including perceptions of its cleanliness, privacy, and convenience. The third contained questions about the household's WTP for improved sanitation facilities. The final part of the questionnaire contained questions about the socioeconomic characteristics of the household, including such items as education, income, ownership of assets, weekly expenditures, occupation, religion, and housing characteristics.

A two-stage stratified sampling procedure was utilised to select a random sample of 1,633 households. Twenty enumerators (16 men and 4 women) were each given one week of intensive training in the administration of the questionnaire. Enumerators were instructed in the precise translation of the questionnaires into the predominant local language (Twi) and were trained in how to ask questions and elicit answers. This training included extensive use of role playing. Each enumerator was observed in practice interviews and was tested on his or her ability to administer the questionnaires. Field supervisors returned to selected respondents after the enumerator reportedly completed an interview in order to verify that the enumerator had, in fact, interviewed the correct household and that the interview had taken place as reported. Each completed questionnaire was checked by a supervisor for omissions and errors, and where problems were found, the interviewer was instructed to return to the household in order to rectify them.

Out of the 1,633 households in the sample frame, usable interviews were completed with 1,224 respondents. The overall response rate for those households that could be located was very high: only 4 percent refused to be interviewed (3 percent of the total number of households). Two percent of the completed interviews were discarded because of inconsistencies in the respondent's answers.

Respondents were asked about their WTP for five different types of sanitation services: Kumasi Ventilated Pit Latrines (KVIPs); water closets (WCs) with sewer connections; sewer connections for households already with WCs and septic tanks; private water connections; and both a private water connection and a WC with a sewer connection for households currently without water. Each household was not asked its WTP for all five levels of service but only for those relevant to its particular circumstances. For example, if a household had a water connection but did not have a WC, it was possible to ask the respondent about its WTP for both a WC with a connection to a sewer and a KVIP. If a household already had water and a WC, it was not relevant to ask how much they would pay for a KVIP; rather, the researchers asked how much the household would be willing to pay to connect the WC to a sewer.

The enumerators described each of the relevant options by reading from a prepared text, and, for some of the options, by showing diagrams and pictures to the respondents. A combination of 'YES/NO' questions and a direct, open-ended question was used to elicit the respondent's maximum WTP (this question format is termed an 'abbreviated bidding procedure with follow-up'). The respondent was first asked whether or not he would choose to pay a stated monthly fee for one of the specified technologies. In order to test whether respondents' answers were sensitive to the questionnaire design, the starting value of this initial fee was varied among respondents: some received a high starting value and others received a low value. A respondent who received a high starting value for one level of service or technology also received a high value for all subsequent levels of service in the interview.

The iterative bidding procedure had three steps, depending on whether the respondent received a high or low initial value (see Table 3.1). This question format was used for each of the five services. The order of the questions about different services was the same for all respondents.

Both tenants and landlords were interviewed, and somewhat different introductory statements were required for each. In addition to the different versions for landlords and renters, for households with and without water, and for high and low starting points, the questionnaire was also designed to test whether one subset of respondents (renters with water) bid differently if they were given one day to reflect before giving their answers to the WTP questions. In total, ten different versions of the household questionnaire were administered in the field. Which version a specific household in the sample received was randomly assigned; the enumerators had no control over it.

Table 3.1 Iterative bidding procedure

	Low Starting Value		High Starting Value
1	Ask initial starting value; if NO, go to (3), if YES go to (2)	1	Ask initial starting value; if No, go to (2), if YES go to (3)
2	Increase the initial value to the high starting value, and ask if respondent is willing to pay; then go to (3)	2	Decrease the initial value to the low starting value, and ask if the respondent is willing to pay; then go to (3)
3	Ask respondent for the maximum amount he is willing to pay for the service described	3	Ask respondent for the maximum amount he is willing to pay for the service described

3.2.3 Results of the analysis

Table 3.2 presents means and standard deviations of households' WTP bids (based on the follow-up, open-ended question) for the five types of service for groups of households with different existing water and sanitation conditions. As shown, households without a WC on average said that they were willing to pay about the same amount per month for a WC as for a KVIP (US$1.40 vs. US$1.45). Households with a WC said they were willing to pay slightly less than this for a connection to a sewer (US$1.30). On average, households without water connections said that they were willing to pay US$1.52 for a water connection and US$2.57 per month for both a water connection and a WC. This result suggests that the demand for water and sanitation is largely additive; that is expenditures for one do not substitute for the other.

Households with private water connections but without a WC were asked their WTP for both a KVIP and a WC with a sewer connection. On average, they were willing to pay about 7 percent more for a WC and sewer than for a KVIP. There were large differences in the mean WTP bids for KVIPs between households with water using public latrines and households with water using other sanitation systems. For example, households using public latrines were willing to pay about 37 percent more for a KVIP than households with bucket latrines, which makes sense because households using public latrines are the most dissatisfied with their existing sanitation system and are currently spending the most on sanitation.

Table 3.2 Average household willingness-to-pay for improved sanitation services based on existing water and sanitation situation

	Willingness-to-Pay (US$/month) for:				
Existing Sanitation	KVIP	WC and Sewer	Sewer Connection	Water	WC Water
Households with water					
Bucket latrine	1.13 (0.92)	1.24 (1.01)	...	...	...
Public latrine	1.55 (1.13)	1.66 (1.16)	...	...	...
Pit latrine	1.23 (0.92)	1.26 (0.90)	...	...	...
WC	...	...	1.31 (1.06)	...	...
Other	1.34 (0.62)	1.19 (0.62)	...	...	...
Households without water					
Bucket latrine	1.49 (1.03)	...	...	1.71 (1.73)	2.60 (1.59)
Public latrine	1.72 (0.98)	...	...	1.61 (1.20)	2.72 (1.74)
Pit latrine	1.15 (0.82)	...	...	1.13 (0.76)	1.78 (1.16)
Other	1.33 (1.02)	...	...	1.32 (0.91)	2.07 (1.30)
Overall Mean	1.45 (0.92)	1.40 (0.95)	1.30 (0.98)	1.52 (1.01)	2.57 (1.42)

Note
Values in parentheses show the standard deviations.

Three different types of multivariate models were used to analyse the relationship that describes the determinants of the WTP bids. Ordinary least squares (OLS) was used to explain the WTP bids obtained in response to the follow-up direct question. The information on WTP obtained from respondents' answers to the 'YES/NO' questions was analysed in two ways. First, a respondent's answer(s) were interpreted as defining interval estimates for his WTP. In other words, the respondent's WTP was assumed to fall into one of the three categories defined by the high and low starting points.

The second method used to analyse the responses to the 'YES/NO' questions was an ordered probit model. This approach assumes that the responses to the questions only provide an ordering of the preferences of respondents. In other words, if one respondent answered the WTP questions with a low bid and another respondent answered with a high bid, the only information that is assumed to be obtained from these responses is that the first respondent was willing to pay less for the improved sanitation service than the second respondent. Each of these three approaches to the multivariate analysis progressively relaxes the assumptions about the precision of WTP information that can be obtained from the contingent valuation survey for improved sanitation services.

All three multivariate modelling approaches use the same four types of variables for explaining variation in WTP bids for a given sanitation technology:

1) characteristics of the questionnaire (for example whether a respondent was given a high or low starting point, or time to think);
2) characteristics of the respondent (for example sex, education);
3) socioeconomic characteristics of the household (for example income); and
4) household's existing water and sanitation situation.

Overall, the multivariate results from all three modelling strategies were remarkably robust and consistently showed the same independent variables being statistically significant. The results showed conclusively that the WTP information obtained from the contingent valuation survey for all five levels of improved service is systematically related to the socioeconomic characteristics of the household and the respondent in ways suggested by consumer demand theory and prior expectations. This is true regardless of the source of WTP information (that is answers to the 'YES/NO' questions in the bidding game or the open-ended final question); the estimation method used; or the exact model specification.

The four explanatory variables with the consistently largest effects on WTP have clear economic interpretations: household income; whether the respondent owns the house or is a tenant; how much the respondent's household was spending on its existing sanitation system; and how satisfied the respondent was with his household's existing sanitation system. Households with higher incomes bid significantly more for all types of improved services than households with lower incomes. Owners bid much more for improved service than tenants, indicating a greater willingness to invest in their own property. Respondents who were paying more for and who were dissatisfied with their existing sanitation service bid more for improved sanitation services (both KVIPs and WCs with sewer connections) than respondents who were paying less and were more satisfied.

Perhaps the most surprising finding of these multivariate analyses is how little effect any of the social or cultural variables had on individuals' WTP for improved sanitation or water services. More educated respondents generally bid more than less educated respondents, but this effect is statistically significant in only a few of the models and its magnitude is always small. The gender of the respondent and whether the respondent is the head of household are almost never statistically significant, and the direction of these effects is mixed. The only case in which the age of the respondent influences WTP is for WCs with sewer connections: older respondents bid less for this type of sanitation improvement than younger individuals.

The experimental design incorporated numerous tests to check the internal consistency and reliability of the households' WTP responses, including a test for starting point bias, a 'time-to-think' effect, and the effect of observers listening to the interview. These tests revealed little reason for serious concern about the reliability or accuracy of the WTP responses.

The authors do not argue that households' WTP bids accurately reflect the public health benefits of improved sanitation in Kumasi because they do not believe that households are fully aware of the health risks to which they are currently exposed by their existing sanitation practices. The WTP bids do, however, appear to reflect households' perceptions of the value of improved sanitation options.

3.2.4 Discussion

This research provides additional evidence that contingent valuation surveys can be successfully conducted in cities in developing countries and that useful information can be obtained on household demand for public services such as sanitation. The multivariate analyses of the WTP responses compare very favourably with similar analyses carried out in industrialised countries.

From a policy perspective, the results of the study indicate that conventional sewerage is simply not affordable to the vast majority of households in Kumasi without massive government subsidies. In retrospect this is perhaps not so surprising. What was less apparent before this research, however, was the widespread acceptance of KVIPs and the approximate levels of subsidy which would be required to achieve different coverage goals with a KVIP subsidy program. The results of the CV survey showed that most households were willing to pay about as much for a KVIP latrine as for a WC connected to a conventional sewerage system. The study also indicated that households' WTP for water and for sanitation appear to be approximately the same order of magnitude and largely separable.

The authors show that if loans were available at a real interest rate of 10 percent for 20 years, essentially no subsidies would be necessary to install KVIP latrines in Kumasi. In other words, if households could engage in financial transactions under terms considered to be more or less normal in industrialised countries, households' WTP for improved sanitation would be sufficient to pay the full costs of KVIPs. The authors do not suggest that public authorities should intervene in the financial markets to solve the sanitation problem or offer subsidised loans for the construction of KVIP latrines, but rather point out that household WTP for KVIP latrines was in fact quite substantial. It just would not buy much in the capital market conditions prevailing in Kumasi in 1989.

3.3 Travel Cost Method: Valuing Eco-tourism in a Tropical Rainforest Reserve

Tobias, D. and Mendelsohn R. (1991), 'Valuing Eco-tourism in a Tropical Rainforest Reserve', *Ambio*, **20** (2), pp. 91–93.

3.3.1 Introduction
In many countries forest loss often results from the perceived value of the forest resources relative to alternative land uses, particularly agriculture. Prescriptions for forest conservation therefore stress the need to recognise the resource's total economic value. In other words, forests are worth more than their timber. A comparison of relative returns should account for the variety of priced and non-priced goods and services frequently produced, even if these are difficult to quantify. As deforestation accelerates there has been a surge of interest in high profile uses such as the harvest of secondary forest products and tourism. Tobias and Mendelsohn attempt to quantify recreation value applying a zonal travel cost method to domestic visits to the Monteverde Cloud Forest Reserve (Costa Rica). In so doing, they attempt to demonstrate the economic value visitors assign to their visit over and above the price they already pay to access the reserve.

Their finding that the inferred tourist valuation of the reserve can potentially exceed the economic value of the competing alternative land use by a magnitude up to two times is indicative of a current bias in economic appraisal which largely ignores non-market benefits.

3.3.2 Fieldwork and data collection

Costa Rica is one of a number of countries with environmentally sound and carefully planned tourism (mainly to its protected areas). Located between 8 and 11 degrees north of the equator, a diverse terrain combined with tempering Pacific and Caribbean climatic influences assures a high biodiversity rating in a relatively small area. Although wealthy relative to many of its Central and Latin American counterparts, land conversion to agriculture – mainly coffee, bananas and livestock – is a constant threat to the country's diverse ecological environments which include 24 National Parks. As is the case in many other developing countries, there is a need to justify resource commitments which are perceived to have a high opportunity cost. Protecting areas for the sake of biodiversity alone is rarely a convincing justification for forgone development benefits. The case for eco-tourism therefore needs to be convincing and provide a demonstrable return to the country.

The travel cost method infers the value users place on a recreational experience from their travel behaviour. Tobias and Mendelsohn use the zonal variant which begins with the collection of address information of domestic visitors to the 10,000 hectare private reserve. Visitors are assigned to a zone according to their canton (state) of origin and an average visitation rate for each zone is calculated by dividing observed visits by canton population. Next, zonal average visit cost is estimated. A composite cost estimate is derived based on a standard cost per kilometre (distance measured between the reserve and the main town of each canton), out of pocket costs, a fraction of fixed costs (that is wear and tear) and a value of travel time. The authors do not specify the fraction of the hourly wage rate they use to value travel time, but do emphasise the sensitivity of the final result to these initial cost assumptions. A total of 81 observations (corresponding to the number of cantons) are available to estimate a demand function relating visitation rate to price (travel cost) plus extra available data on canton population density and literacy which are thought to affect observed visitation rates.

3.3.3 Results of the analysis

For each canton (observation on the price, that is cost, axis) a measure of the total consumer surplus is derived from the area above the price line and below the fitted demand curve. This is essentially a measure of the difference visitors from a zone paid to get to the reserve and how much the demand curve indicates they would be willing to pay. Note that the latter assertion is based on the strong assumption that visitors from all zones have identical tastes with respect to the site, and react in the same manner with respect to costs. After calculating the consumer surplus for each canton, the authors sum over all cantons to obtain an annual consumer surplus of between US$97,500 and US$116,200 depending on the constituents of the estimated function (and thus the slope of the curve).

It seems reasonable to suggest that Monteverde Reserve is unique and that its conversion would signify a loss of the estimated surplus in perpetuity. The true economic value of the reserve should thus be represented by the present value of this stream of annual benefits. As time goes by, however, the supply of rainforest reserves is likely to decrease, and thus the value of protected areas like Monteverde will increase. Rising demand and reduced supply of substitute sites implies increased visitation rates and a higher consumer surplus. The authors therefore suggest that simply to discount the future stream of benefits by a factor r would underestimate the value of the site by discounting distant benefits at too great a rate. Using a growth rate a as a proxy of the increasing visitor value, a net factor $(r - a)$ of these offsetting rates is taken as the appropriate factor to adjust benefit streams. The derivation of this factor is not discussed by the authors who opt for a rate of 4 percent to translate the estimated consumer surplus perpetuity for Monteverde to a present value of between US$2.4 and US$2.9 million. (The authors do indicate that visitation to the reserve had grown 15 percent a year for the five years prior to 1988, such that the net discount factor may be negative.) Alternatively dividing the annual consumer surplus estimate by the number of domestic visitors in 1988 yields a value of around US$35 per person.

The estimated values do not include foreign visitor valuation of the reserve. The authors suggest that it is reasonable to assume the domestic valuation as a lower bound valuation by a foreign visitor who travels further and has fewer alternatives at home. On this basis the addition of foreign visitors increases the estimated present value of the rainforest reserve to a range of US$2.5 and US$10 million. Opting for US$8 million a value per hectare of US$1,250 is obtained by dividing over the 10,000 h^2 of the reserve.

3.3.4 Discussion

How useful is this per hectare valuation? Conservation of Monteverde competes with agriculture in surrounding areas. The market price of agricultural land can often be interpreted as representing the present value of everything that can be produced on it over time. A current price of land outside the reserve of between US$30–$100 per hectare therefore compares unfavourably to the per hectare recreational present value of US$1,250. In other words, conversion to agriculture would incur an economic cost per hectare at least equal to the difference between the two options. Conversely the expansion of the reserve represents a well justified investment from an economic and social perspective. Including other non-priced elements such non-marketed forest products and biodiversity values may further increase the return to conservation.

There are several caveats to the presented estimates, many of which are related to problems inherent in the travel cost approach. As already indicated, the authors note the sensitivity of consumer surplus estimates to the assumptions underlying the composite cost per kilometre. Small changes to any of the elements that make up this cost affect the slope of the estimated demand curve and therefore estimated consumer surplus. The estimates of economic benefits are also sensitive to the assumed value of time spent travelling to the site. This debate hinges on the rationale that leisure time should be valued less than remunerated labour time or even at zero if the opportunity cost so dictates. A related problem alluded to in the paper, is that the benefit estimate derived from the demand curve relates to the whole trip experience and not just the on-site recreational benefit. The assumption of an identical consumer surplus for domestic and foreign visitors to Monteverde to calculate the aggregate visitor consumer surplus range, seems unlikely. Foreign visitors may incur great cost getting to Costa Rica and have few areas similar to Monteverde nearer home. It is unlikely though that foreign visits are for a single purpose and therefore erroneous to assign the whole travel cost to any single site. Although the authors have assigned a conservative value to foreign consumer surplus, the issue of multipurpose visits needs to be understood to avoid seriously biased benefit estimates.

While it is clear that methodological difficulties noted here need to be further addressed, the current study begins the task of quantifying missing forest values. Only as methods and measurement become more robust will the true value of forest resources be truly appreciated and possibly captured by their owners.

3.4 Hedonic Pricing: Willingness-to-Pay for Water in the Philippines

North, J. H. and Griffin, C.G. (1993), 'Water Source as a Housing Characteristic: Hedonic Property Valuation and Willingness-to-Pay for Water', *Water Resources Research,* 29 (7) pp. 1,923–1,929.

3.4.1 Introduction

Billions of dollars are invested every year in potable water supply projects in urban and rural areas of developing countries, but only rarely are these investments subjected to serious economic analysis. In the past the international donor community and national governments in developing countries have assumed that potable water supply systems – particularly in rural areas – must be subsidised because most households are too poor to pay for improved water systems. Most donor agencies and national governments thus exempt water supply projects from the kind of economic analysis routinely applied in other sectors. This scepticism about the role of economic analysis is deep-seated among professionals working in the water supply sector, most of whom are doubtful that balancing the costs and benefits of a water supply project is a useful exercise.

There are two principal reasons for this scepticism. First, many sector professionals believe that clean water should be provided as a basic right, or that it is a 'merit good' that should not be subjected to economic analysis. Second, sector professionals doubt that the economic benefits of water supply projects can be determined with sufficient accuracy for the estimates to be useful for practical purposes. Until recently, there has in fact been surprisingly little empirical work on the economic benefits of water supply projects.

This paper illustrates that it is feasible to use an indirect, non-market valuation technique to estimate the economic benefits that result from improved water supply projects. The authors use the hedonic property valuation method to determine how imputed household rental values in one large rural area of the Philippines reflect households' WTP for the different types of water supply services (private connection in the house, a tap in the yard, or a communal source) and distance to the source. The results of this paper are consistent with a growing body of empirical evidence that suggests that people in developing countries are willing to pay substantial amounts for reliable, high quality water supplies in their home. The economic benefits of improved water supplies are likely to be especially large in peri-urban communities where households are already purchasing the majority of their water from vendors. The economic benefits in rural areas of developing countries where water vending is not present are typically much lower.

3.4.2 Fieldwork and data collection

Data for the analysis came from a 1978 survey of 1,903 households in a 14,000 square kilometre area of the Bicol region, one of the poorest parts of the Philippines. The sample was chosen randomly and was designed to be representative of the region in terms of population and income distribution. The data were collected as part of a health policy project, not specifically to estimate a hedonic property value model.

About 90 percent of the sample owned their own homes, and only a quarter of the remaining 10 percent reported paying rent. For the purposes of the authors' analysis, the renters were dropped from the sample. The head of the household was asked to estimate the value of the dwelling, not including any valuation of the land that a household might own surrounding the residence. Monthly rent was imputed as one percent of the reported value of the structure.

The Bicol survey included an extensive list of questions about all possible sources of cash or 'in-kind' income. The authors used a human capital formation model to estimate the permanent income of each household in the sample. These estimates were used to place households into three income categories used in the analysis.

Information from the survey that was used to describe characteristics of the dwelling included water source, number of bedrooms, quality of construction materials, and location. The sample respondents used six primary water sources:

1) a private connection in the house supplied by a community system;

2) a private connection in the house supplied by the household's own pumping system from a deep well;
3) a tap in their yard supplied by a community water supply system or household's own pumping system;
4) public tap;
5) shallow well with water raised by bucket;
6) traditional water source (for example spring, lake or river); and
7) other (purchased water or rainwater collection).

The authors used three variables to characterise a household's water situation. The first is a qualitative variable for whether the residence had piped water in the house; the second is a qualitative variable that designated whether a household had a deep well with water pumped into the house or yard. Although only three percent of the households in the sample had access to a private water connection with water supplied from a public system, 30 percent were able to approximate this level of service by paying the cost of drilling a deep well on their property and self-supplying. Relative to a public tap or traditional source, the authors hypothesised that each of these would add to the perceived value of the dwelling.

The third set of information regarding water source that the authors used in their analysis was distance to the water source used by the household, which was expected to be negatively correlated with the value of the dwelling (and thus to imputed rent). There was only modest variation in the distance to the water source for households in the sample. About 75 percent used a water source within 50 metres of the house; 22 percent carried water from distances over 75 metres.

The authors measured the construction quality of the dwelling by creating an index of construction materials. The index took a value of one if the house was made of straw or similar material, a value of two if the house was made of a mixture of straw and cement or wood, and a value of three if it was made entirely out of wood or cement and had a metal roof. Size of the residence was expected to be positively related to imputed rent. Distance to the nearest town in kilometres was expected to be negatively related to rental value.

3.4.3 Results of the analysis

The hedonic model is based on the idea that households choose to rent or purchase a house based on dwelling and community characteristics. A bid–rent function can be formulated that characterises the trade-offs each household is willing to make between attractive characteristics of the dwelling and community, and paying more rent. Regressing the monthly rental value of a dwelling on its characteristics, such as water source, construction materials, number of rooms, and lot size, yields an estimate of the hedonic price function. Marginal WTP for each characteristic is the derivative of the hedonic price function with respect to that characteristic. However, only if consumers are all alike would these simple estimates realistically characterise each household's WTP.

The authors' approach to this latter problem is to divide the sample into three different income groups, and to estimate a bid–rent function directly for each group. This approach assumes that households in each income group have similar tastes. The problem is formulated as a random utility model in which the bid–rent parameters are estimated by predicting the type of household likely to occupy a particular house. The modelling approach used by the authors allows them to estimate directly the bid–rent function without having to recover the parameters of the utility function.

The authors estimated households' WTP in terms of the capitalised value of improvements to water situations. The households in the sample pay monthly costs associated with the use of different sources. These costs take the form of water charges, electricity, and household members' time. The attached table presents the parameter estimates of the discrete choice bid–rent approach. These coefficients can be interpreted as the marginal WTP for each housing characteristic, assuming that tastes are similar within each of the three income groups. Ignoring the intercepts, 13 of the 18 coefficients are significant at or above the 10 percent level for a two-tailed test; most of these are significant above the 1 percent level.

The model results in Table 3.3 show that the coefficients of the non-water characteristics generally behave as hypothesised. 'Number of bedrooms' is significant and positive for middle and upper-income households, but not for the low-income group. Low-income households are willing to pay more, however, for greater proximity to the main town. The middle-income group will not pay anything to be closer to town; the higher-income group will pay to be farther away from town. All income groups are willing to pay more for a house constructed of better materials.

Households in all income ranges are willing to pay about half of their monthly imputed rent to have piped water in the house supplied by a public system. WTP for piped water in the house works out to US$1.95 per month in 1978 for higher income households, US$2.25 for middle-income households, and US$1.41 for low-income households. These amounts are in addition to the monthly costs of using these services (including any existing water tariffs). The poorest households are not willing to pay more for water in the yard or house if it is supplied by the household's own well. Middle-income households would pay about US$0.94 per month for the capitalised cost of this option and high-income households would pay about US$0.88 per month for it.

The authors also examined the question of how much households value greater proximity to a communal source. Somewhat surprisingly, they found that WTP for a closer water source was statistically significant only for higher-income households. Even for high-income households, the magnitude of the effect of distance on WTP was small. This may have been because few households were collecting water from long distances from their home.

Table 3.3 Results of bid–rent estimations (dependent variable is imputed monthly rent)

Discrete Bid–Rent: Mean Hedonic Price or Bid–Rent			
Variable	Lower Income	Middle Income	Higher Income
Intercept	−25.924 (5.52)	−46.243 (10.87)	−47.321 (11.02)
Piped water in the house (0 = no, 1 = yes)	10.427* (1.70)	18.130* (3.85)	15.486* (3.31)
Deep well water into the house or yard, or a yard tap (0 = no, 1 = yes)	−2.147 (0.57)	6.948* (2.42)	6.459* (2.25)
Distance to water source	0.001 (1.10)	0.0002 (0.18)	−0.004* (2.19)
Number of bedrooms	2.194 (1.38)	7.967* (6.21)	11.290* (9.77)
Distance to central town	−0.834* (5.81)	0.011 (0.51)	0.396* (2.04)
House materials	9.863* (4.18)	12.734* (5.98)	10.321* (4.97)
Scale parameter		0.044 (123.96)	

Notes
The *t* statistics are given in parentheses.
* Indicates significance at or above the 10 percent level for a two-tailed test. The model as a whole is significant at better than the one percent level using a likelihood ratio test.

3.4.4 Discussion

The analysis presented in this paper shows that the housing market in this poor, rural area of the Philippines does place a value on water source and that it is capitalised in the price (imputed rental value) of the house. The authors found high WTP for piped, in-house water from community systems by all income groups and somewhat lower WTP for water in the yard. These inferences were relative to the excluded communal source. There was almost no measurable WTP for greater proximity to a communal source.

This finding suggests that a project that either reduces the distance to, or improves the site of, a communal source would have negligible value to most households. However, a project that provided individual house connections would significantly increase wellbeing.

The authors compared their estimates of households' WTP for water supply improvements with cost estimates for water supply systems in the Philippines. They concluded that WTP is probably not adequate to cover the capital cost of piped water systems either in the house or yard.

3.5 Contingent Valuation: Water Quality in Barbados and Uruguay

McConnell, K.E. and Ducci, J.H. (1989), *'Valuing Environmental Quality in Developing Countries: Two Case Studies'*, Paper presented at Allied Social Science Association, Atlanta, Georgia.

3.5.1 Introduction

For much of the period when economists have worked actively on projects and policies in developing countries, the value of services from the environment was ignored. This treatment of environmental services was explained by appealing to the suspected high income elasticity of demand for such services. People with low incomes simply would not pay for environmental services. Several alternatives may explain the occasionally observed low level of environmental quality. For example, the market failure may have not revealed the demand for environmental services.

However, the good and bad environmental consequences of development projects have become increasingly apparent. And increasingly, development agencies seek to measure the economic costs and benefits of these externalities. For development projects which will alter the quality of a resource or the environment, contingent valuation methods have special appeal because they enable researchers to measure the benefits in cases where there are no sources of secondary data or no observable behaviour to exploit.

This paper reports on studies conducted in 1988 and 1989 in two countries in Latin America using contingent valuation methods to measure the value of improvements in water quality. These studies were originally designed to evaluate projects, not to do research on contingent valuation. This paper is concerned with the kinds of problems that arise in doing contingent valuation on environmental problems in developing countries.

3.5.2 Contingent valuation for the Barbados sewer system

The project in Barbados, an island country in the Caribbean, involved a study of the benefits and costs of the construction of a sewer system along with collector lines. The system, designed for the south coastal area of Barbados, would require households, non-profit organisations, and businesses to hook up to the lines proposed for construction. The collector lines would feed a plant which would provide primary treatment for waste water. This treated water would then be piped out through a gap in the fringing reef. The system is planned for a small area of Barbados.

For households, the sewer system would potentially provide environmental services. In the sewer district, households currently dispose of their waste water into the subsurface. For some households, the disposal of waste water into the ground creates occasional problems, such as overflows, and filled septic tanks among other things. However, most households do not suffer any immediate consequences. Barbados is a coral island and the soil has great permeability. The permeability means that waste water gets to the groundwater and into the ocean relatively rapidly. It is contended that the absence of a sewer has two effects: it pollutes the water used for swimming on the south coast beaches (via higher coliform) and it destroys the fringing coral reefs which surround the island. The coral reefs are apparently impaired by the excess nutrients. Some scientists maintain that there is a secondary effect from the dying reefs. These reefs provide protection for beaches from open ocean waves, and the death of reefs may induce additional beach erosion. However, there is currently not strong evidence that the major beaches in the area are polluted although it is contended that coliform counts in the marine waters are occasionally high around large hotels. These beaches are heavily used by residents and tourists and appear to be clean.

Thus the installation of a sewer system potentially creates three kinds of direct services: easier disposal of waste water; cleaner water for swimming and beach use and expected healthier reefs; and knowledge of a healthier marine environment. There is also a potential indirect effect. If the marine waters gain a reputation of being severely polluted, tourist activity, essential to the economy, may be reduced, bringing a decline in employment. However, the environmental returns are in a sense counterfactual. They can be imagined, given the continuing pollution from waste water. But there is currently little evidence (and little perception) that the beach waters are polluted. Those households who live in the sewer district stand to receive all three services, while those who live outside the district will only enjoy service flows from a healthier environment. Consequently, two different contingent valuation studies were carried out, one for households who live in the sewer district and one for the rest of the households in Barbados.

The contingent valuation survey for households in the proposed sewer district was preceded by two focus groups and several pilot surveys of draft questionnaires. The survey was administered by a firm in Barbados with personnel quite familiar with sample survey techniques. Both the small size of the island and the difficulties with phone or mail techniques suggested the use of in-person interviews. The interviewers were elementary school teachers. They were trained in the technical issues of sewer systems and water quality as well as in the nature of the interview process.

The questionnaire for the households who live outside the sewer district asked only about the environmental aspects of the sewer system. The instrument proceeds by asking a limited set of questions on household characteristics. It then explains briefly the implications of the sewer system. Households are told the potential impact of disposing of waste water into the ground, and the potential of avoiding polluted beach water and damaged reefs by construction of the sewer system.

Then the respondent is offered two choices:

1) pay a randomly varied increase on the quarterly water bill to achieve the aims of the sewer system; or
2) not pay and continue the path of potentially polluting the beaches and other environmental consequences of private disposal of waste water.

In responding to this question, households who do not live in the sewer district are being asked to assess the effect of continued disposal of waste water into the ground, and the impact of this disposal on marine water quality. Unless they perceive a connection between water quality and the sewer system, they do not stand to gain.

A two stage sample of households and districts resulted in 432 observations of households for this second referendum. The interviewing was conducted by interviewers who were trained for this questionnaire but who had previously been employed on national censuses for population and economic purposes. Part of the training included attending focus groups where the details of the questionnaire were worked out.

To complete the analysis, a model of the responses was estimated. The following model demonstrates the fitting of the responses for households not in the sewer district:

$$\text{Probability (yes to the question)} = a_0 + a_1 d + a_2 age + a_3 ctv - b_y w \quad (3.1)$$

where d = 1 if household visited relevant beaches more than 15 times a year;

d = 0 otherwise;

age = age of respondent;

ctv = 1 if household had seen a television show about the relation between the sewer system and pollution of Barbados beaches;

ctv = 0 otherwise; and

w = 4 (increment to quarterly water bill).

The water bill is multiplied by four to convert to an annual figure. The water bill and all subsequent monetary measures are in local dollars, which exchange two to one for US dollars. The ctv variable represents an increment to knowledge about the sewer system and its impact on the marine environment.

The estimated model in general agrees with prior notions about the utility of waste treatment. Utility is higher in the 'with-the-sewer-system' case for people who use the beaches frequently or who have seen a television show which describes the impact of the sewer system on water quality. (The impact of the ctv variable suggests that there is currently little perception of impaired water quality.) Utility is lower for older people or when a higher charge must be paid. The age variable works because older people tended not to believe that the marine waters could be polluted.

This model can be used to calculate the sample WTP for constructing the sewer system. The general expression for this WTP is:

$$Ew = (a_0 + a_1 d + a_2 age + a_3 ctv)/b_y \qquad (3.2)$$

For the parameter estimates from Equation 3.1, the expected WTP, assuming that the parameters are known constants, is:

$$Ew = (1.04 - 0.0279 age + 0.3996 ctv + 0.6118 d)/0.0097 \qquad (3.3)$$

This model implies a mean WTP for the sample of US$11.

The households in the district where the sewer system is to be installed were given a similar referendum, but one that included the services of public waste water disposal. The interview asked a series of questions about the household characteristics and water disposal. Households were given a description of the sewer system and its role in preserving clean water and protecting coral reefs. The randomly chosen households were offered the choice of:

1) paying a randomly varied quarterly addition to their water bill and receiving the services of waste water disposal, cleaner beaches and other environmental amenities; or

2) not paying the increment to the water bill and continuing the private method of waste water disposal and continuing the threat to the environment.

In contrast with the households outside the sewer district, these respondents need not understand the scientific connection between the sewer system and marine water quality. Some households can anticipate receiving direct benefits from the installation from connecting to the sewer system.

A random sample of 277 households was drawn from the approximately 3,200 households in the sewer district. The following model is representative of those households with the potential to connect:

$$\text{Probability (yes to the question)} = c_0 + c_1 d + c_2 age + c_3 ctv - d_y w \quad (3.4)$$

where the variables are the same as for the referendum for the households outside the district except that $d = 1$ for households who visit the relevant beaches anytime during the year and zero otherwise.

Estimation of this model showed that it is stronger than the model for households outside the sewer district in several senses. The mean WTP to install the sewer system is:

$$Ew = (1.057 - 0.0207 age + 0.8744 ctv + 0.6748d)/0.00216 \quad (3.5)$$

The mean WTP is US$178.

There is some reason for suspicion based on results from households who live in the sewer district. The respondents were asked a series of questions about whether they had problems with their disposal of waste water. For a test of whether households who had problems would be willing to pay more, a dummy variable, 'problem' was created. This variable, which took a value of one when the household suffered one of a series of problems that confront people when they are not hooked up to a sewer system, was not significant and did not impact the parameter estimates. The insignificance of this variable is a troubling reminder that respondents may not be considering all the information available to them.

3.5.3 A system of collector lines in Montevideo, Uruguay

The third contingent value study of interest here involves the construction of lines disposing of waste water in Montevideo, Uruguay. About 80 percent of the households and businesses in the area are connected to sewer lines. But the lines run into main lines, which are drained directly into the estuarine water of the Rio de la Plata which surrounds the city. The waste water flows directly into waters adjacent to the municipal beaches. The project involves collecting the waste water at the mouth of the drainage pipes into one main outlet pipe and shipping the waste water well out into the estuary. There would be no primary treatment, simply disposing of the untreated water far enough out to eliminate the pollution of the immediate beaches.

In contrast to the Barbados case, the residents of Montevideo are well aware the water is polluted. Households are frequent users of the beaches. Municipal bus lines regularly pass popular beaches on their routes. And many residential neighbourhoods are within easy walking distance of various beaches. Local awareness of the beach pollution arose from extensive publicity surrounding the beaches in 1985. During that time, the level and meaning of the faecal coliform counts at various beaches became a subject of television and local papers. The coliform counts were quite high. The average for all sites for a study in 1978 was about 5,000 per 100 ml. For some sites the average was over 80,000 per 100 ml. In contrast, beaches in Chesapeake Bay, United States are closed when the count goes above 500 per 100ml.

The specific project to be analysed in Montevideo concerned the second phase of the sewer project. The first phase, collector pipes for beaches along the eastern part of the Montevideo shoreline, is ready for construction. The beaches to the east are far more popular. They have better sand and wave characteristics. The second phase concerns collectors to the west of Point Carreta. The project involves installing more collectors, after the beaches to the east have been cleaned up. However, the benefit–cost analysis must be done before the initial project is completed and its effects felt on the water quality. Consequently, the contingent valuation must be of a conditional sort. The referendum questions deal with WTP for the second project, requiring the respondent to assume that the first project is completed. The respondent is given the following introduction to the referendum:

As you know, the beaches of Montevideo are contaminated. Suppose that the beaches to the east of Point Carreta are cleaned up enough to allow swimming and other water activities.

The respondent is offered the following choices:

1) pay a randomly varied additional amount for municipal taxes and obtain cleaner water for the beaches west of Point Carreta, assuming that the beaches east have already been cleaned up; or
2) not pay the additional tax and continue to have highly polluted water in the beaches to be cleaned up by the second phase of the project.

The relevance of the first and second stages is simply the impact of substitutes on consumer surplus. When a good has easily accessible substitutes, its elasticity will be greater and its consumer surplus less. When the eastern beaches are clean, the demand for cleaning up the western beach will be less and the WTP for making it cleaner also less.

The questionnaire was given in person to 1,500 randomly sampled households in Montevideo. The questionnaire underwent testing with a focus group and pilot testing of several versions of the questionnaire. The instrument was administered to household heads by experienced interviewers who were employees of a well known survey company.

The model shows how responses to the question were fitted to a relationship:

Probability (yes to the question) $= e_0 + e_1 y + e_2 dwest + e_3 d + e_4 age - l_y w$ (3.6)

where y = 1 if household income above the low income level;
    dwest = 1 for households who are planning to use beaches in the western area in the future;
    d   = 1 if the household is a beach-going household;
    age = 1 if household head is less than 60 years old;
    w   = randomly varied municipal tax.

This model squares well with intuition. The impact of the proposed payment is negative and strongly significant. Age, income status and being a beach-going household increase the chance of saying yes. The dummy on planned future use of the western beaches, the ones to be cleaned up by the project, is also strongly significant.

The WTP is calculated as:

$$Ew = (e_0 + e_1 y + e_2 dwest + e_3 d + e_4 age)/l_y \qquad (3.7)$$

Using the parameters estimated from Equation 3.7, the mean WTP is US$14 per year. This is less than one percent of the median family income. Depending on how individuals view the future, this may be low by the standards of Barbados. It may represent some strategic behaviour induced by the vehicle of a municipal tax. The tax seemed a natural vehicle, but feedback from the interview process suggested that it was an unpopular option.

3.5.4 Discussion

Contingent valuation studies in Barbados and Montevideo, Uruguay have estimated the WTP for installing various components of a sewer system. In Barbados, the WTP for the lifetime of services was estimated to be US$178 while in Uruguay, the annual WTP was estimated to be US$14. There is no particular reason why they should be equal, because the services they are purchasing are different. However, at a personal discount rate of 7.86 percent they are equal. These results require a number of caveats, and one should generalise cautiously. Nevertheless, there are some insights to be gained from these studies.

First, do these studies provide evidence that households in these countries value environmental quality? The studies address the benefits of an improvement in environmental quality and this improvement is valued in most cases because environmental quality is complementary to the recreational commodity consumed by the household. That is, the improvement is valued by the individual for its contribution to utility, and it will not necessarily provide increases in real money income. The answer to this question, which is of course conditioned on one's faith in these particular contingent valuation studies, is affirmative. There are two sorts of evidence. First, in all three studies, households exhibit a mean WTP for the environmental services. The second sort of evidence comes from the estimated models. Despite the conditional and uncertain nature of the environmental effect, the two cases share some promising characteristics. The surveys were not designed to test for strategic bias. But there is evidence that the hypothetical nature of the questions did not render the responses purely random. Responses in both fitted models are significantly influenced by access and economic characteristics in expected ways. Random responses would not be significantly related to regressors. However, the explanatory powers of the models, in terms of pseudo R^2s is low, ranging from 0.23 to 0.10. Thus, there is much about the responses that is not explained.

Some details of the estimated models are systematic. Each model shows that beach users are willing to pay more for the improvement than households who do not use the beach. This specific result, basically an implication of weak complementarity, stems from the significance of d, the beach-going dummy, in each equation. In a broad sense, people respond to the referendum questions as if they have preferences for environmental improvements, and these preferences are compatible with what we expect from the simplest economic theory.

Several temporal aspects of contingent valuation studies arise in project analysis in developing countries, and have not been faced by most CV users in the US. One of these is the time pattern of the payment. In very large projects such as sewer systems, the present discounted value of the costs is quite high. Only in a well functioning credit market are households indifferent between different paths of payments which have the same discounted value. In many developing economies, credit markets are highly imperfect. One stream of payments is not equivalent to the discounted value of another stream. And because the costs are so high and credit markets so imperfect, households would all reply no to a referendum that queried them about a range of cost figures centred around the mean present discounted cost of the project.

This temporal issue leads to another. Since most households will not pay the present discounted value of the mean cost, the payment must have a time element. For example, the question may ask the household head whether she/he would pay an increment to the water bill for the next three years. Or the question may involve an increase in taxes indefinitely. This time path of payments requires some assumptions about the household's temporal preferences. An even more troublesome problem occurs in countries where the rate of inflation has been historically high. For example, in Uruguay, the annual inflation rate in consumer goods was about 70 percent when the survey was conducted. With high and persistent inflation, people are quite sophisticated about the real value of payments at different times. In such settings, the researcher needs to develop a method to fix the price level at which the respondent evaluates the proposed payment. We can expect that anticipated inflation and personal time preferences will be embodied in the respondent's answers.

The absence of market data and the need to value environmental components of projects in developing countries will put pressure on researchers to use and improve contingent valuation methods for valuing environmental quality. One of the difficulties for lending agencies stems from the modest success of the trials discussed here. If these studies had failed, then it would be easy to say the method does not work. But there is no evidence of failure, in the sense of outlandish implied results of the model or inability to administer the questionnaire. Typically, contingent valuation research has been directed towards improving the method, testing the sensitivity to various forms of payment, checking for bias by varying the questions in an experimental design, and so forth. Further, there is a growing sense of how to do such studies. But what a lending officer needs is a way to ferret out bad studies from good ones, *ex post*. For example, the statistical analysis of why people answered yes, no, or refused to respond could prove insightful.

3.6 Opportunity Cost Approach and Contingent Valuation: Forest Functions in Madagascar

Kramer, R.A.., Sharma, N., Shyamsundar, P. and Munasinghe, M. (1994), 'Cost and Compensation Issues in Protecting Tropical Rainforests: Case Study of Madagascar', *Environment Department Working Paper*, World Bank, Washington DC.

3.6.1 Introduction
Tropical countries in Africa are putting greater emphasis on management and protection of intact rainforests. Preservation of tropical rainforests has significant social, economic, and environmental impacts. Protecting forests gives rise to benefits in terms of conservation of biodiversity and maintenance of environmental services, but there are also negative impacts borne by people living adjacent to protected areas who depend on these forests for their livelihoods. Often traditional use rights to the forest are lost when large areas of tropical rainforests are protected or converted to other uses.

Development projects have often failed to take into account the opportunity costs of people with traditional rights to forests where large forest areas are protected or converted to other land use activities. The failure to adequately compensate or involve people in the establishment and management of protected areas has resulted in poor performance of many projects dealing with reserves and natural parks. In many instances, these parks and reserve areas are vulnerable to open access problems from local populations.

This study analyses the economic and social impacts of establishing the Mantadia National Park in Madagascar on village households living adjacent to tropical rainforests in the Andasibe region. Two methods are used to estimate the economic impacts on the villagers: opportunity cost analysis based on household cash flow models constructed from a socioeconomic survey; and contingent valuation analysis based on direct questioning of villagers about required levels of compensation.

The Mantadia National Park does not have any human settlements within its boundaries, but has villages in close proximity, mainly in the south, east and north east. These villagers are dependent on the forests within the park and immediately around it for forest products and for agriculture. The primary source of livelihood in these areas is shifting cultivation, a major cause of deforestation in the park area. Villagers in this area are also dependent on the forests for a number of other reasons. Fuel wood is collected from the forests on a regular basis, a wide variety of fish and animals are foraged for consumption and a number of different types of grass are harvested and used for assorted purposes. Forest plants and herbs also serve as sources of medicine.

3.6.2 Fieldwork and data collection

In order to assess the extent of the dependence of villagers on the forests, a socioeconomic survey was conducted of 351 households living near the park. The survey included a series of questions on economic activities related to use of agricultural land, the forest, and household labour. An additional component of the survey was a contingent valuation exercise to assess villagers' willingness-to-accept (WTA) compensation for loss of access to the park.

This survey was accomplished with the assistance of a local Non-Governmental Organisation (NGO) well versed in rural survey techniques. The household survey was refined based on focus group interviews, conversations with various people who were well acquainted with the area, and a pretest which covered about 25 households. In addition, a shorter questionnaire was administered to village leaders to obtain information on village history, agriculture, and land use practices. To increase the villagers' willingness to participate in the survey, a health team of doctors and nurses was organised to accompany the survey team. The health team provided basic medical consultations and medicines to the villagers who have very little access to health services.

To estimate the opportunity cost to villagers of establishing the Mantadia National Park, cash flow analysis was used. Income from agricultural and forestry activities was estimated for three different groups of villages. The villages were grouped to reflect similar socioeconomic characteristics. Then depending on the extent to which land in the park had been used by villagers for gathering forest products and practising shifting cultivation (based on analysis of aerial photographs of the park), estimates were made of the income losses associated with the loss of access to park land.

Each of the three cash flow models measured the economic benefits from the forests within the park to the locals if they continued to have access to the park. (This is the 'without park' scenario.) The regulations under which the park has been formulated indicate that the villagers will not be allowed to use the area within the park for shifting cultivation or forest product harvesting (the 'with park' scenario). The cash flows, therefore, estimate the value of land to the average household assuming a 'without park' scenario. This value is equivalent to the opportunity cost of establishing the park to the average household. Monte Carlo simulation was used to examine the effects of fluctuations in key variables on the cash flows.

The second valuation method used in this study was the contingent valuation method (CVM). The CVM questions used a WTA format. The pretest conducted suggested that while property rights over forested land are held by the state, the people in this region have been using forest resources for a long time, and they perceive that they have traditional rights to the land. WTA seemed not only the most appropriate format to use, but also the only way to obtain meaningful responses.

Because several of the villages surveyed had limited involvement in the cash economy, the numeraire used in the survey to obtain WTA bids was rice. Rice is the main crop in this region and its value is well understood. Furthermore, some amount of rice is also sold or bartered, and transactions of rice are thus known and understood by the local people. The unit of measure used was a 'vata', which is a locally-used unit for rice transactions, equalling 30 kilogrammes (kgs) of rice.

Prior to posing the contingent valuation question, the respondents were asked a series of questions prompting them to begin thinking about the benefits drawn from the park. These questions probed perceptions on different aspects related to the forests like flooding, soil erosion, ancestral traditions, wildlife as destroyers of crops, availability of primary forests in the future, and so on. Respondents were also asked if they knew about the park and about their perceptions on the use of buffer zones as alternatives to the forests in the park. The contingent valuation question used was:

Suppose you are asked to use only the buffer zone set aside for collecting forest products and for growing crops and are asked not to use the rest of the forests any more. Suppose in order to make up for asking you not to use the forests in the park, you are given _____ vata of rice every year from now on. Would this make you as content as before when you could use the forest in the national park?

Respondents were randomly assigned to seven groups, corresponding to different amounts of rice used as the offered bid levels.

3.6.3 Results of the analysis

The household survey covered a total of 17 villages lying to the east and south of the Mantadia region. The total population covered by the household survey was 1,598; average household size in this region is 4.6 persons. Most of the villages do not have access to any medical facilities, running tap water, or electricity. The village children in general suffer from malnutrition. Malaria, chest congestion-related illnesses, and venereal diseases are other significant health problems affecting this population. In general, most of the villages surveyed either had or were within 4–5 kilometres from primary school facilities. However, the survey indicated the average number of years of education per person to be only 2.4 years.

Rice production is the primary economic activity in the area. The average household produces 487 kgs of paddy rice per year worth about US$128. Most households also engage in shifting cultivation. Eighty percent of the households surveyed said that they would add to existing land for cultivation. Other crops grown are maize, beans, manioc, sweet potato, taro, sugar cane, ginger, banana, and coffee.

Based on the data collected on agricultural and forestry inputs and outputs, the cash flow models were used to estimate the opportunity costs borne by the villages as a result of lost access to the forests in the park. Averaging over the results obtained from the three cash flow models, the mean value of losses was US$91 per household per year (Table 3.4). Aggregating over all households living in the vicinity of the park and using a 10 percent discount rate and twenty year time horizon, the net present value of the opportunity costs was estimated to be US$566,000.

Table 3.4 Summary of economic analysis of Mantadia National Park

Estimates of economic losses to local villagers from establishment of Mantadia National Park		
Method used	Annual mean value per household	Aggregate net present value
Opportunity cost	$91	$566,000
Contingent valuation	$108	$673,000

The contingent valuation responses were analysed with an econometric model. The discrete choice responses were used to estimate a bid function in a logistic regression framework. The estimated bid model revealed that a number of socioeconomic variables were systematically related to the probability of accepting offered bids. The bid level itself was a positive and significant explainer of responses. The model correctly predicted 86 percent of the responses, clearly indicating that the elicited responses were non-random. From the estimated bid function, a mean bid was calculated. The responses to the contingent valuation questions indicate that on average, a compensation of rice equivalent in value to US$108 per year per household would make households as well off with the park as without (Table 3.4). Aggregating over the population in the park area, this implies a necessary one time compensation of approximately US$673,000 assuming a 10 percent discount rate and twenty year time horizon.

3.6.4 Discussion

The Mantadia National Park has been established with the intention of preserving Madagascar's unique biological heritage. While the benefits of conserving the fauna and flora and the biological diversity within the park are large, some very significant opportunity costs must be considered, as a necessary condition, to avoid open access problems that will threaten the existence of the park in the long run. Approximately 3,400 people in three sets of villages will be negatively affected by the park. The results suggest that an annual compensation of approximately US$100 per household would be required. Such compensation could be made in the form of education, health facilities, alternative income earning enterprises in the buffer zone, or other development activities. These compensation costs appear to be a significant part of the true cost of implementing protected area projects and should be built into project design at an early stage. Without adequate compensation and active cooperation of local residents, natural resource management projects are more likely to fail.

The cash flow approach used in this study is a relatively simple, but data-intensive form of analysis. It is a powerful tool for understanding the interrelationship among microeconomic factors relating to use and management of parks. In this study, contingent valuation was also used to estimate the welfare change perceived by local residents as a result of loss of access to lands currently within the Mantadia National Park. The analysis indicates that CVM, rigorously applied, can be effectively used in the developing country context. The econometric analysis undertaken indicates a systematic association between various socioeconomic variables of interest and the expressed WTA compensation. Also, the opportunity cost (or market based) approach and the CV method provided remarkably comparable estimates of costs borne by villages. All this is encouraging evidence to support the use of CV in such a context, but further research is required to improve its widespread applicability.

Several lessons can be drawn from this study. This research has involved a survey of village households, collection of data on various quantities and prices, and rigorous quantitative analysis. Research of this kind is time intensive. It is apparent that there is a strong need for a significant amount of pre-survey work to draft a useful survey instrument. There is a need for focus groups and a formal pretest to sharpen the wording of the questions so that the desired information can be collected. For example, it was found that units of measure for forest products varied between villages only a few kilometres apart. There is a need for involving local sociologists and cultural anthropologists (as was done in this study) who can ensure that the questions are posed appropriately for the local cultural context, and to advise researchers on the appropriate protocol for approaching local village leaders to ensure their cooperation. In this instance, it was found advantageous to provide an incentive for survey participation by arranging to have a health team accompany the interviewers. Of course, careful translation into local languages is also a necessary step, as is thorough training of interviewers. The study team worked with an experienced rural survey group, but found that extensive training was still necessary. This was in part due to the fact that they were unfamiliar with the contingent valuation method. Despite the considerable effort required to collect the data gathered for this village study, this information is critically important for implementing conservation projects, and can be collected when baseline information about residents within or around conservation areas is gathered.

3.7 Random Utility Model: Water Supply in Pakistan

Altaf, M.A., Jamal H., Liu, J.L., Kerry Smith, V. and Whittington, D. (1991), '*A Random Utility Model for Connections to Public Water Systems in Developing Countries: A Case Study of the Punjab, Pakistan*', Working Paper, Department of Economics, North Carolina State University.

3.7.1 Introduction
Water utilities typically need a high percentage of households to connect to a piped water supply system so that revenues are sufficient to cover capital and operating costs. In industrialised countries the vast majority of households that are offered the option of connecting to a piped water supply system choose to do so, and such households usually use water from this piped system as their sole source of supply. In many developing countries this is not the case. For a variety of reasons, many households decide not to connect to piped water systems and, even if they do, also use other sources of water. Sound water supply planning in

developing countries thus requires an understanding of the factors that influence a household's decision on whether or not to connect to a piped water system.

Little systematic empirical research has, however, been undertaken on this subject. Water supply planners often simply assume that a household will connect to a piped water system if the monthly tariff is less than 3–5 percent of income. This rule of thumb has proved to be a poor predictor of household behaviour. This paper reports the first economic analysis of a household's decision to connect to a public piped water supply system based on a behaviourally consistent theoretical framework. A random utility model (RUM) was used that described the connection decision as a discrete choice: whether to connect or not to an existing public water system. This model considered the effects of cost factors and demographic and attitudinal variables on these decisions. Because the model is consistent with constrained utility-maximising behaviour, it was also used to estimate households' consumer surplus from piped water connections.

3.7.2 Fieldwork and data collection

The data used in this research came from 378 household interviews conducted in five villages in the Punjab, Pakistan. All of the villages had piped water systems. Some households had decided to connect, and others had not. These connection decisions took place over a fourteen year period. Connection involved multiple costs for a household: a one-off connection fee, the private cost of connecting to the distribution line and installing the associated indoor plumbing; and a monthly tariff. The prices faced by households varied with each village, as well as with the time they made their decisions.

The five study villages were located in two districts of the Punjab: Skeikhupura and Faisalabad. Historically, public open wells were the primary source of drinking and cooking water in both districts. Over the last couple of decades, both districts have experienced a transition in households' water supplies: community wells have been replaced by private hand-pumps inside the home. For villages in the Sheikhupura (or 'sweet water') district, groundwater is readily available and is universally perceived to be of good quality. The Faisalabad district has experienced the same transition to private hand-pumps as the Sheikhupura district, but the Faisalabad district has poor quality ('brackish') groundwater. Here 54 percent of the households with the option to connect to a piped system rely on water sources other than groundwater from private hand-pumps for their drinking and cooking water. In the Faisalabad district water from private hand-pumps is used largely for washing and for animals. Some households in both districts (nearly 20 percent in Sheikhupura and 50 percent in Faisalabad) have electric motors to pump water into an overhead tank for distribution throughout the house via indoor plumbing.

A house connection to a piped water system is considered to be an increment to a household's existing hand-pump (and/or electric motor) systems for water in the home. For households in the sweet water district, a private connection to a public water supply system allows installation of indoor plumbing for those without electric motors, and it may improve the reliability of their overall water supply. In the brackish district a private connection will provide the same opportunities to introduce indoor plumbing and improve overall reliability, but it will also provide high quality drinking and cooking water in the home.

Piped water systems have been available for different lengths of time in each of the villages in the sample. In the sweet water district, the average time was about twelve years. In the brackish district, one village in the sample had a piped water system introduced only seven months before the survey. Respondents were asked in the survey when their household connected (if they had) and the prices and costs incurred at that time. Because households connected at different times and the nominal tariffs and connection fees were largely constant for each system, the real prices households paid to connect varied considerably because of general inflation. This change in real water tariffs and connections fees allowed the authors to observe how connection decisions were influenced by the relative prices of access to piped water.

The personal interviews were administered in the Punjabi language to an adult male, usually the head of the household, during March and August, 1988. The surveys collected information on each household's economic and demographic profile and patterns of water use, as well as other information about their attitudes and valuation of public piped water supplies. Because tariff collection and cost recovery practices in the study villages were erratic, in most cases the authors used household reports for the three components of the costs of connection: the tariff (and the frequency with which it was collected); the connection fee paid at the time of connection; and the costs to bring the water from the distribution line into each house. For some households the officially stated terms for the tariff and connection fees were used.

While the cost of bringing water from the distribution line to the house would be known by households connecting, non-connecting households might be expected to have incomplete information on these costs. In the survey these households were asked to estimate these costs. The cost estimates provided by connecting and non-connecting households were each regressed on the distances respondents reported for the distance from the distribution line to their homes. Actual costs were found to bear a strong relationship to distance, while estimated costs did not. The authors assumed that all of the households faced the same cost function per metre for these services and used distance as a measure of this component of the connection cost. Both the monthly tariff and the connection cost were deflated using the International Monetary Fund's consumer price index for Pakistan.

3.7.3 Results of the analysis

Probit models were used to explain the households' decisions on whether or not to connect to the piped water systems as a function of the costs of connection, socioeconomic and demographic characteristics of the household, respondents' attitudes, and the households' existing water supply situation. The results indicate that in both districts all three components of costs – the tariff, connection fee, and hook-up costs (as measured by distance) – are statistically significant negative influences on connection decisions. Moreover, as expected, the one-off costs have a smaller effect on the likelihood of connection than the tariffs, reflecting some form of annualisation of these costs over the perceived lifetime of the system.

The model results for the demographic and attitudinal variables offer a number of interesting insights. First, education is a positive and generally significant determinant of the connection decision in both the sweet water and brackish districts. Second, in both districts family size is a positive, significant influence on the connection decision. This is consistent with intuitive expectations.

Third, the measures used to describe the household's labour supply available to collect water from sources outside the home (that is, the proportion of children and women in the household) have quite different effects on connection decisions in the two districts. In the brackish district both the proportion of women and the proportion of children variables are negative influences on the connection decision, but only the latter is statistically significant. In contrast, in the sweet water district the proportion of women and proportion of children variables are positive influences on the connection decision. (The latter is statistically significant in only some of the models.) The negative, significant effect of the proportion of children in the brackish district would be consistent with an expectation that household members not involved in market work would have responsibility for fetching water from alternative supplies.

The models for both districts included a qualitative variable indicating whether a household feels that the government should provide the water supply free. In both cases this has a negative effect on connections, as expected. The models for the brackish district included a variable that indicated whether the respondent felt that metering household water supplies was a good idea. A positive attitude toward metering had the expected positive and significant effect on the connection decision.

The authors used the parameter estimates from the probit models of the determinants of the connection decision to evaluate how the three components of the costs of a piped water supply affected the economic benefits households realised from connecting to piped water systems. To construct consumer surplus measures for access to piped water systems, the authors assumed that the measures correspond to the maximum amount the household would be willing to pay for the service annually, given the terms on which private connections were available in each district. In other words, it was the excess they would be willing to pay over and above the costs of a connection. This corresponds to the annual tariff increment that would make a household indifferent between connecting or not connecting. Estimates of consumer surplus were calculated for each household in the sample.

Table 3.5 reports the results based on the parameter estimates from one of the probit model estimations (the consumer surplus estimates were quite stable over model specifications). Average estimates of consumer surplus are presented for households in both the brackish and sweet water districts and for connecting and non-connecting households. As shown, WTP estimates were approximately comparable across districts. (Note that since prices are different in the two districts, the incremental WTP estimates are measured with respect to different baseline costs). As expected some of the estimates are negative, and more negative estimates result for households that chose not to connect.

3.7.4 Discussion
The findings from this study suggest that household demand for piped water supplies in developing countries can be effectively modelled using a random utility framework. In this specific application, both one-off connection costs and monthly tariffs were found to influence connection decisions. The study results showed a difference in the effect of one-off connection costs and monthly tariffs on household connection decisions.

The authors emphasise the policy importance of any difference in the time horizon and rate of time preference between the water authority and the household. If the water authority and the household do not have similar planning horizons and discount rates, then household welfare can be improved simply by adapting to this difference. For example, if the water authority has better access to capital markets than rural households, there is scope for arbitrage based on the differences in annualisation adjustments between the water authority and households. In practice, this would mean that the water authority should borrow to provide financing for households to pay connection fees and connection costs over time.

For example, if it is assumed that the water authority considered its time horizon to be indefinite (that is greater than 70 years) and faced a 10 percent real rate of discount, then an annual tariff of 10 rupees would be equivalent, from the water authority's perspective, to a fixed charge of 100 rupees. To determine whether their model results indicated an opportunity for arbitrage, the authors considered this kind of information in relation to what a household perceives as equivalent changes in its fixed versus annual charges. Their model results for households in the sweet water district suggest that the implicit annualisation of capital charges makes one-off connection charges a more significant deterrent to connection than the tariff. The results for households in the brackish water district suggest the opposite.

Table 3.5 Estimates of annual household consumer surplus for connection to piped water system (in 1985 rupees)

	Annual Consumer Surplus* for households that...	
	connected to a piped water system	did not connect to a piped water system
Sweet water district		
Mean	78	26
Min	−0.6	−38
Max	282	108
Standard Deviation	54	30
N	121	61
Brackish water district		
Mean	43	19
Min	−21	−94
Max	133	54
Standard Deviation	24	24
N	148	50

* The calculations for these estimates of consumer surplus used the individual household characteristics and reported values for all variables except the tariff. For both districts the tariff was set at the average value. For the sweet water district this was 102 rupees per year, and for the brackish district this was 119 rupees per year.

The authors argue that in order to correctly evaluate alternative water pricing policies, one must consider the importance of tariffs versus one-off charges, a household's time horizon, rate of time preference, and borrowing and lending rates in local credit markets, as well as these same issues from the perspective of the water authority. Available studies in industrialised countries on how households evaluate one-time capital charges versus continuing tariffs imply high rates of discount to 'rationalise' *ex-post* observed decisions. However, from the perspective of a decision maker in the water authority, the time preferences of different households should be considered largely unknown. In this case a strong argument can be made that the water authority should offer households financing for one-off connection charges at a non-subsidised rate. If some households choose to accept this offer, the water authority has provided these customers a valuable service: these households benefit from the transaction and the water authority has not incurred any costs to itself.

3.8 Contingent Valuation: Water Quality in the Philippines

Choe, K. Whittington, D. and Lauria, D.T. (1995), '*Household Demand for Surface Water Quality Improvements in the Philippines: A Case Study of Davao City*', The Environment Department, World Bank, Washington DC.

3.8.1 Introduction

Until recently, the conventional wisdom in the development community has been that most people in developing countries do not put a high value on improvements in environmental quality, either because they are unaware of the problem or because they cannot afford to pay for it. It was thus argued that investments in such areas as water pollution control either had to be postponed until per capita incomes were substantially higher, or would have to be heavily subsidised by central government.

The wisdom of the latter course, that is subsidies, was generally questioned by economists, who believed that the benefits of such investments were likely to be small because environmental quality improvements were a low priority for poor households.

However, over the last few years environmentalists and many members of the development community have questioned whether investments in environmental quality improvements should wait until incomes rise. They have argued that economic development and improvements in environmental quality are in fact complementary, not competing objectives. This argument that environmental quality should not be sacrificed for economic growth was the principal message of the United Nations Conference on Environment and Development in Rio de Janeiro in 1992.

This paper examines the question of the magnitude of household demand environmental quality improvement in the context of a specific proposal: the clean up of the river and sea near Davao City, Philippines.

Davao City, the second largest city in the Philippines, is located on the island of Mindanao. The city is primarily in a strip of coastal plain alongside the Gulf of Davao. The Davao River and other rivers and streams run through Davao City into the Gulf. Most households have water-sealed toilets for their exclusive use; these empty into septic or holding tanks. Less than 1 percent of the population of Davao City is connected to a sewage collection system; the few small existing systems service a handful of upper income subdivisions. Mean monthly household income in Davao City was about 5,100 pesos (US$204) in 1992.

Davao City has great potential for both domestic and foreign tourism. There are many beautiful tropical beaches located on several small islands in the Gulf of Davao, and numerous beach resorts have been built on these islands for picnicking, fishing, snorkelling, and overnight stays. However, these island resorts are too expensive for the majority of the population of Davao City. Until 1992 most residents of Davao City used the local beaches very near the urban areas, the most popular of which was Times Beach. Travel time to Times Beach is only about 10 minutes by bus or taxi from most parts of Davao City. The sea at Times Beach is polluted by the nearby discharge of the Davao River, which carries silt, storm water drainage, and household and industrial waste water from the Davao City. Human waste from coastal squatter settlements near the mouth of the Davao River also contributes to the pollution.

In the past literally thousands of residents of Davao City would use these nearby local beaches for picnicking and swimming on weekends. However, in early 1992 the City Health Department found very high levels of faecal coliforms and pathogens in the water and issued a series of warnings to the public about the health risks of swimming at the beach. There was much publicity in the local media about this problem, and most people stopped using Times Beach. In November and December 1992, a contingent valuation survey was carried out to determine how much households in Davao City would be willing to pay for improved water quality in nearby rivers and the sea; these improvements would result in increased recreational opportunities and possible public health improvements for residents of Davao City.

3.8.2 Fieldwork and data collection

In order to implement the contingent valuation survey, thirty individuals from local universities and government agencies were trained to administer household questionnaires. All were experienced in conducting household surveys in Davao City or neighbouring areas. Three faculty members from the University of Mindanao, all with survey experience, were hired to supervise these enumerators.

The household questionnaire itself was developed over a two-week period of intensive collaboration with the enumerators and field supervisors. The enumerators and field supervisors actively participated in decisions on which questions to include and their wording and translation. Interviews were conducted in Cebuano. Numerous focus groups were held to discuss water pollution problems. Several pretests of the questionnaire were carried out with about 200 households before the questionnaire was finalised.

All of the versions of the survey instrument included an introductory section with questions about the household's and respondent's demographic characteristics followed by five basic parts. The first and second parts focused on the household's existing water and sanitation situation, and its level of satisfaction with these services. The third part sought information on the respondent's priorities for environmental improvements, use of beaches near Davao City, and knowledge and level of concern about water pollution problems. The fourth part included questions about the household's WTP for improvements in water pollution problems if these were offered at different prices. Finally, the fifth part of each questionnaire included questions about the socioeconomic characteristics and housing conditions of the household.

A referendum question was used to measure household demand for water quality improvements. Respondents were asked to assume that there was a city-wide plan to clean up the rivers and sea and make Times Beach safe again for swimming. They were not told specifically what this plan would entail. Households were told that if this hypothetical plan were adopted, each household would be required to pay a monthly fee and that industries would also do their fair share to reduce waste water discharges to the river. Respondents were then asked to vote on whether their household would support such a plan at the specified monthly price. Different monthly fees were randomly assigned to different households. Households with private water connections were told that this monthly fee would be added to their water bill.

A total of 581 in-person interviews were completed with respondents throughout Davao City in which this kind of referendum question was asked about a city-wide plan to improvement water quality. The overall response rate was 65 percent. Thirty two percent of the households in the sample could not be located by enumerators. Only 3 percent of the total number of households in the sample refused to be interviewed.

3.8.3 Results of the analysis

Statistical methods were used to examine how respondents' answers to the referendum questions were influenced by different randomly assigned monthly fees. Figure 3.1 shows the relationship between the probability of the respondent voting for the city-wide plan for improving water quality and the monthly fee proposed for two different assumed distributions of the responses (Weibull and log-normal). As illustrated, for both assumed distributions, the support for the water quality improvement plan falls sharply as the monthly fee increases. At a price of 25 pesos per month (US$1), one half of the sample households would support the plan. At a price of 50 pesos per month, 25 percent of the households would vote for the water quality improvement plan.

Multivariate techniques were used to see how respondents' answers to the referendum questions were related to socioeconomic characteristics of the household and to estimate the mean WTP of different types of households. The results show that household WTP for water quality improvements is low, both in absolute terms and as a percentage of income. Not only was household WTP for improved water quality low in Davao City, but 15 percent of the respondents refused to pay anything at all.

Several results from the research suggest that these low estimates of WTP for surface water quality improvements are likely to reflect respondents' true preferences. First, the statistical analysis of respondents' answers to the referendum questions unambiguously indicate that the respondents' answers to the first referendum question asked depended on the monthly price offered. For example, not a single respondent who was offered the plan for 200 pesos per month voted for it. These results suggest that the estimates of household WTP are not likely to be biased by respondents agreeing to pay prices they cannot afford.

Second, the results of multivariate analyses of the determinants of the responses to the referendum questions show clearly that households with higher incomes are willing to pay more for environmental improvements than households with lower incomes. If the income of the average respondent in Davao City were to double, household WTP for water quality improvements would increase by about 20 percent. Also, households that used Times Beach were willing to pay about 30 pesos per month (about 0.6 percent of mean household income); non-users were willing to pay almost nothing. Such findings provide further evidence that respondents considered their personal circumstances and budget constraints when answering the WTP questions.

Third, these low estimates of household WTP are consistent with information collected in the household survey about households' social and environmental attitudes and priorities.

The answers respondents gave to attitudinal questions concerning environmental priorities confirm that reducing water pollution is not a high priority for residents of Davao City. When asked to select their first priority for government action from a list of eight environmental problems, less than 10 percent of the respondents selected water pollution in rivers and along the seashore. (This is true even for households living near the sea and along the river.) Although water pollution is not perceived to be a pressing problem, people are aware of water pollution problems and have taken action to avoid the risks associated with this environmental contamination. For example, a large majority of respondents reported that the water quality of the sea near Davao City had become 'much worse' and that the 'suitability of the sea near Davao City for swimming and bathing' had become 'much worse' over the last twenty years. Over 90 percent of the respondents said that they had heard about pollution problems in Times Beach. Eighty percent of the respondents said that they had not gone swimming or bathing at Times Beach since the public health alert, and almost 40 percent of these respondents said that the reason they had not been to Times Beach in the past year was because it was too dirty. About 10

Figure 3.1 Probability of household supporting water quality improvement plan (Scenario 1) versus. monthly fee

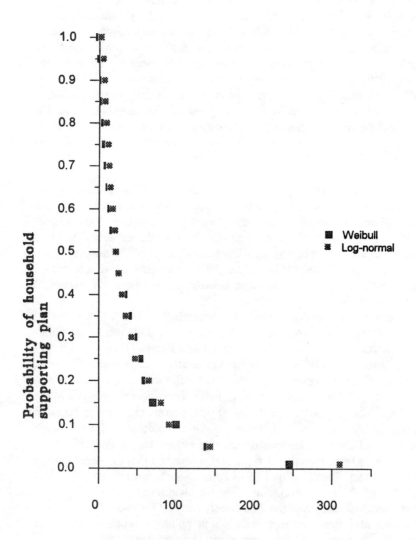

Monthly fee for Water Quality Improvement Plan (pesos)

percent of the sample respondents reported that they do not eat seaweed or shellfish collected from the sea near Davao City because of concerns about contamination.

3.8.4 Discussion

When WTP for pollution abatement is low, it is often argued that subsidies are required due to the presence of externalities and lack of knowledge of public health risks. In Davao City these arguments seem less compelling. The externalities associated with lack of waste water treatment do not fall on downstream communities but largely on the residents themselves. Thus the damages from water pollution are largely borne by the community creating the problem and are thus already 'internalised'. Moreover, the reason WTP is low is not because households are unaware of the problems caused by water pollution. Indeed, many residents of Davao City have already changed their behaviour significantly to avoid the risks of water pollution. This finding suggests that public education campaigns or social marketing efforts designed to increase household demand for water quality improvements are not likely to have a dramatic effect on WTP.

The analyses of the data collected in this contingent valuation survey in Davao City confirm the conventional wisdom about household demand for environmental improvements in developing countries. Water pollution control is simply not a high priority of residents of Davao City; households are willing to pay very little of their income for water quality improvements and beach clean up, both in absolute terms and as a percent of their income.

People do feel that they have lost valuable recreational opportunities as a result of water pollution, and many are concerned about possible food contamination. But these are not major problems in their lives compared to other more pressing concerns. Because households' WTP for water quality improvements in Davao City is much lower than the costs of providing such improvements, and because most households feel that other environmental problems such as deforestation and poor solid waste collection and disposal deserve higher priority, the appropriate strategy appears to be to wait until incomes are higher and WTP has risen before embarking on a large water pollution control investment program.

3.9 Production Function Analysis: Afforestation Benefits in Nigeria

Anderson, D. (1987), '*The Economics of Afforestation: a Case Study in Africa*', Johns Hopkins University Press; and Anderson, D. (1989), 'Economic Aspects of Afforestation and Soil Conservation Projects', in Schramm, G. and Warford, J., '*Environmental Management and Economic Development*', Johns Hopkins University Press, Baltimore, pp. 172–184.

3.9.1 Introduction
Careful examination and measurement of the environmental benefits of afforestation can greatly increase the 'economic rate of return' to forestry investments. One study in northern Nigeria assessed the benefits of afforestation in northern Nigeria as:

1) halting the future decline of soil fertility (since trees typically reduce soil erosion);
2) raising current levels of soil fertility;
3) producing tree products – fuel wood, poles, fruits;
4) producing fodder both from raised productivity of soils and from forest fodder.

3.9.2 Methodology
The methodology involved tracing each of the uses of local forests and valuing the relevant outputs at market or shadow prices. Thus, the leaves of the trees in the forest provided fodder for livestock. The fodder was collected for 'free' or could be sold in the market place. The value of the fodder could therefore be estimated directly by looking at market prices, or indirectly by estimating the effect of the fodder on livestock weight and hence livestock value. Not all forest benefits can be related so directly to market values, however. The trees in the agroforestry systems act as windbreaks, thus raising crop productivity. However, there is then no obvious market in that windbreaks are not bought and sold in the marketplace. But provided the resulting increase in crop productivity can be estimated, the economic value of the trees can be estimated via the effect on the output, and hence on the money value of crops.

3.9.3 Results of the analysis
The net present values (NPVs) and economic rates of return (ERRs) that resulted for shelter–belts (planting trees mainly for wind protection) and farm forestry (intermixing trees and crops) are given in Table 3.6. Calculation of timber costs and benefits alone in the Kano area have tended to show rates of return of around five percent, which has to be compared with the desired or target rate of return which is usually much higher, at around ten percent. In other words, afforestation does not pay. But once the other benefits are included, economic rates of return are much more attractive.

Table 3.6 Net Present Values (NPVs) and Economic Rates of Return (ERRs)
resulting from afforestation schemes

	Shelter-belts		Farm forestry	
	NPV	ERR	NPV	ERR
Base case	170	14.9	129	19.1
Low yield, high cost	110	13.1	70	14.5
High yield	221	6.2	–	–
No erosion	108	13.5	75	16.6
More rapid erosion	109	13.6	60	15.5
Soil restored + yield jump	263	16.9	203	21.8
Wood benefits only*	–95	4.7	–14	7.4

* Wood and fruit for farm forestry.

3.9.4 Discussion
The analysis shows that counting 'wood benefits' only produces negative net present value and correspondingly low economic rates of return. But if allowance is made for the effects of trees on crop yields, and for expected rates of soil erosion in the absence of afforestation, the picture is transformed for both farm forestry and shelter-belts.

3.10 Production Function Analysis of Health Costs of Air Pollution in Brazil

Seroa Da Motta, R., and Fernandes Mendes, A.P. (1993), *'Health Costs Associated with Air Pollution in Brazil'*, Working Paper, Applied Economic Research Institute (IPEA), Rio de Janeiro, Brazil.

3.10.1 Introduction
The air quality in many cities in developing countries has deteriorated dramatically over the last few decades, and many efforts are currently being considered to address this problem. There are, however, very few estimates of the economic benefits that would result from air quality improvements in developing countries. Not only are there few estimates of the economic value of air quality improvements, but there are also few studies of the effect of air pollution on human health in developing countries.

This paper first presents an analysis of the relationship between air pollution in San Paulo and mortality rates. This dose–response relationship is then used in an analysis of the health care costs associated with air pollution in San Paulo and in two other Brazilian cities (Rio de Janeiro and Cubatao).

3.10.2 Data collection

The analyses presented were based on secondary data available from several sources. Brazilian environmental law regulates emissions of particulate matter, carbon monoxide, ozone, sulphur dioxide, nitrogen oxide, nitrogen dioxide, hydrocarbons, and methane. (Concentrations of total particulate matter in San Paulo average 140 $\mu g/m^3$, well above the primary national air quality standard of 80 $\mu g/m^3$.) Daily times series data were available from the Environmental Sanitation Technology Company (Companhia de Tecnologia de Saneamento Ambiental) for particulate matter and sulphur dioxide at eleven air quality monitoring stations in San Paulo; for carbon monoxide, ozone and nitrogen oxides at two stations. Because of the low number of deaths per day by district and subdistrict, a quarterly average of each of the air pollutants was calculated from daily air quality reports.

Data on mortality rates and average educational levels of residents in San Paulo were obtained from the State Data Analysis System Foundation (Fundacao Sistema Estadual de Analise de Dadaos) by district and subdistrict for the period 1983–1991. Data were also collected on the number of hospital beds by sanitary district and subdistrict in San Paulo. Data on the average number of hospitalisations per death and the average cost of hospitalisation for respiratory system diseases were obtained from the Integrated Strategic Series Statistical Treatment System (Sistema Integrado de Tratamento Estatistico de Series Estrategicas).

3.10.3 Results of the analysis

Statistical analyses were first done to examine the correlations between levels of various air pollutants. There was a strong correlation between the nitrogen compounds (NO_x, NO, and NO_2). A moderate correlation was found between carbon monoxide and nitrogen monoxide. With regard to the other pollutants, the correlations were not found to be significant. Based on these results, the authors decided to focus their analysis of the relationship between air pollution and health effects on five pollutants: inhalable particulate matter (PM_{10}), carbon monoxide (CO), ozone (O_3), sulphur dioxide (SO_2), and nitrogen dioxide (NO_2).

Two linear regressions analyses were conducted relating death rates from respiratory diseases to air quality, social and economic, and meteorological variables. Education was used as a proxy for all socioeconomic differences in residents in the different districts and subdistricts in San Paulo. The first regression analysis related the death rate from respiratory diseases in a district or subdistrict to particulate matter and sulphur dioxide. The results showed that particulate matter (PM_{10}) was a statistically significant determinant of the death rate from respiratory disease, but that sulphur dioxide was not. The authors note, however, that for most of the period over which data were available, San Paulo was in compliance with sulphur dioxide ambient standards and that sulphur dioxide concentrations had fallen over time. The average temperature had a statistically significant and negative correlation with death rates from respiratory diseases.

Based on the coefficients from the first regression, the authors estimated that an increase of 10 $\mu g/m^3$ of inhalable particulate matter implies an average increase in the mortality rate from respiratory diseases of 1.6 percent. These results are consistent with findings from other countries. The authors calculated that a drop in the PM_{10} concentration from 89 $\mu g/m^3$ to the primary standard of 50 $\mu g/m^3$ would reduce the death rate from respiratory disease by about 6 percent.

Second, death rates from respiratory diseases were related to concentrations of carbon monoxide, ozone, and nitrogen dioxide. The authors found a positive and statistically significant relationship between death rates and ozone concentrations. The authors estimated that a 1 percent reduction in ozone concentrations would lead to a 0.23 percent reduction in the mortality rate from respiratory disease.

The authors used the first regression (based on data from San Paulo) to estimate mortality rates from PM_{10} and sulphur dioxide in three other Brazilian cities (Rio de Janeiro, Belo Horizonte, and Cubatao). These estimates were then compared with the actual death rates from respiratory diseases in these cities. Applying the functional relationship from San Paulo to Rio de Janeiro, the authors estimated a total of 1,252 deaths due to respiratory disease in 1984. This was very close to the actual number recorded of 1,273. The results for Belo Horizonte and Cubatao were similar. The authors thus concluded that the dose–response function estimated for San Paulo was applicable to other municipalities with different levels of air quality.

The next step in the authors' analysis was to estimate the health costs associated with air pollution in different Brazilian cities. These costs were assumed to have two main parts: the monetary costs associated with patients' hospital stays due to respiratory diseases resulting from air pollution; and the income lost by people from missed days of work and premature death due to respiratory diseases resulting from air pollution. No attempt was made to estimate the loss in human wellbeing caused by air pollution in terms of discomfort or pain suffered by city residents.

To calculate the hospital costs due to air pollution, the cost of a hospitalisation resulting in a death was multiplied by the number of deaths associated with air pollution. This involved estimating the number of hospitalisations per death and the average length of each hospitalisation. Table 3.7 summarises the authors' estimates of the number of deaths from respiratory diseases associated with air pollution, the hospital cost per death, and the total hospital costs due to air pollution, for Rio de Janeiro, Cubatao, and San Paulo. The total hospital costs resulting from air pollution in San Paulo for 1989 were estimated to be US$785,000.

Table 3.7 Hospital costs per death and total hospital costs due to air pollution, by city

Year	Municipality	Deaths associated with air pollution	Hospital costs per death	Total hospital costs
1984	Rio de Janeiro	40	US$3,775	US$151,000
1988	Cubatao	29	US$4,896	US$142,000
1989	San Paulo	139	US$5,647	US$785,000

The second component of the health costs, the forgone output from morbidity and mortality due to air pollution, was estimated based on the length of hospital stay and the average income of the patient, for different educational levels. The authors also had to determine the mortality rate curve for respiratory diseases due to air pollution using the estimated dose–response function. Data on the average income of the economically active population by education level was used to estimate the output lost from both lost work days and reduced longevity. The authors' estimates of the economic losses from morbidity and mortality due to air pollution are presented in Table 3.8.

Table 3.8 Costs associated with air pollution (US$/yr)

	San Paulo (1989)	Rio de Janeiro (1984)	Cubatao (1988)
Hospital costs	785,000	151,000	142,000
Morbidity costs	351,000	65,000	71,000
Mortality costs (discount rate = 5%)	1,073,000	201,000	725,000
Total	2,210,000	417,000	939,000

By dividing foregone output due to air pollution mortality by the number of deaths associated with pollution from PM_{10}, the authors calculated what they term an average 'statistical life value' for each of the cities studied. In 1989 US dollars, the estimated statistical life value for San Paulo was about US$7,700; US$5,000 for Rio de Janeiro in 1984; and US$25,000 for Cubatao in 1988. The authors report that these estimates are lower than similar calculations for water pollution that they have done.

3.10.4 Discussion
The authors conclude that the health care costs and productivity losses associated with air pollution in Brazilian cities are considerable. They argue that their estimates of the health-related costs of air pollution are necessary for policy deliberations on air quality control options in Brazil. The authors also suggest that these kind of estimates of the economic costs of air pollution are necessary for setting priorities among various environmental problems.

3.11 Production Function and Implicit Willingness-to-pay for Unique Rainforest: Cameroon

Ruitenbeek, J. (1992), 'The Rainforest Supply Price: a Tool for Evaluating Rainforest Conservation Expenditures', *Ecological Economics*, 6 (1) pp. 57–78.

3.11.1 Introduction
Korup National Park lies in Southwest Province, Cameroon. It contains Africa's oldest rainforest, over 60 million years old, with high species endemism. There are over 1,000 species of plant, and 1,300 animal species including 119 mammals and 15 primates. Out of the total listed species, 60 occur nowhere else and 170 are currently listed as endangered. Continued land use changes are putting substantial pressure on the rainforest. The Worldwide Fund for Nature (WWF) initiated a programme of conservation, centred on a management area of 126,000 hectares plus a surrounding buffer zone of 300,000 hectares. A similar programme was initiated for Oban National Park just across the border in Nigeria.

3.11.2 Methodology
Economic valuation of the rainforest's benefits was carried out in order to assist with the process of raising development aid funds to conserve the area. Estimating benefits was done via the production function approach, that is by looking at the individual functions of the forest and valuing them at market or shadow prices.

The forgone forest benefits include timber from potential commercial logging (the 353 million CFA) and some forgone traditional uses of the forest, mainly hunting, that would be forbidden within a designated national park, and which cannot be offset by diverting activity elsewhere (the 223 million CFA). This proscription of traditional uses affects some 800 villagers within the national park boundaries. In the long run, however, other residents, mainly some 12,000 people on the periphery will be able to continue their traditional use of the forest, which they would not be able to do if deforestation continued.

Thus, while one group loses, another, larger group gains (the 354 million CFA). The tourism figure is conjectural and is based on an eventual 1,000 visitors per annum by the year 2000 and their expected expenditure adjusted for the shadow wage rate. The fisheries item is important. Rainfall in the forest feeds several rivers which feed into large mangrove areas rich in fish. The mangroves prosper on the basis of freshwater inundation in high water periods and saltwater in low water periods. If the forest was to disappear, peak flows from the forest would increase and there would be added sediment and less salinity.

Basically, the mangrove swamps would no longer function as the habitat for the rich fish species that make up both the on and offshore fisheries. Since the link between the rainforest and the offshore fishery is less established than the link to the inshore fishery, only damage to the inshore fishery was estimated. This was valued at the market value of fish and, as a check, at the income derived from the fishery.

The flood alleviation benefits were calculated by looking at the expected value of the income losses that would accrue if there was a flood. The soil fertility benefits were based on a broad brush assessment that, if the forest disappeared, cash crop yields would decline by 10 percent.

Benefits of conservation were then compared to the costs of the conservation project plus the forgone timber revenues. Existence and option values were not estimated. The procedure involved estimating direct and indirect use values to the people of Cameroon and then seeing what the existence and option value would have to be in order to justify the project. Since it was thought that the non-use values would mainly reside with people outside the Cameroon, the focus of attention for non-use values was on seeing what international transfers might be needed.

3.11.3 Results of the analysis

The results were as shown in Table 3.9. From the standpoint of the Cameroon, the project appears not to be worthwhile because there is a negative net present value of some 1852 million CFA at 8 percent discount rate, although there is a modest positive net present value if the discount rate is lowered to 6 percent. The issue becomes one of asking whether the rest of the world would be willing to pay 1,852 million CFA (in present value terms) to the Cameroon to reflect option and existence values. One way of testing this is to look at existing conservation transfers through debt-for-nature swaps. Translated into a per hectare basis, the required transfer for the Cameroon is just over 1,000 ECUs per km^2. Debt-for-nature swaps have implied various valuations ranging from as low as 15 ECU per km^2 (Bolivia) to around 1,600 ECUs per km^2 (Costa Rica). Given the high species endemism and diversity of Korup, values of 1,000 ECUs or more would seem justified. The conservation of Korup forest becomes justified in economic terms, and it may be politically feasible provided this transfer actually takes place.

Table 3.9 Benefits and costs to the Cameroon

Costs of conservation project		
	Resource costs	− 4475
	Forgone forest benefits, timber	− 353
	Forgone forest benfits, forest products	− 223
Total costs:		− 5,051
Benefits of conservation project		
Direct use:	Use of forest products	+ 354
	Tourism	+ 680
Indirect use:	Protection of fisheries	+ 1,770
	Flood control	+ 265
	Soil productivity	+ 130
Total benefits:		+ 3,199
Net benefits to Cameroon		− 1,852
Economic rate of return		6.2%
Net benefits if the discount rate is 6%		+ 319

a) Present values, Million CFA, 1989 prices
b) Discount Rate = 8%

The resource costs are based on budgets and plans in the Korup National Park Master Plan, net of compensation payments (which are internal transfers) and other costs regarded as being not attributable to the conservation project.

The implicit minimum requirement for an international transfer (the so-called 'rainforest supply price') was estimated by taking the present value of net costs (the 1,852 million CFA) and dividing by the present value of the area that could be identified as being protected by the conservation project − some 500,000 'hectare years'. This produces the value of 3,600 CFA per hectare per year, or some 1,060 ECUs/km^2.

3.11.4 Discussion

Notable omissions from the study are twofold: no attempt was made to assess the value of the forest to local people over and above its use value; and no attempt was made to estimate the net contribution to CO_2 emissions from deforestation. Both omissions are likely to reduce the net present value deficit shown in the table. But only the former will lower the rainforest supply price because CO_2 benefits are likely to attract a negligible if not zero WTP on the part of Cameroon citizens. The CO_2 benefits will, however, make it more likely that the rest of the world will pay for rainforest conservation (that is it affects the rainforest demand price).

4. Guidelines for Economic Valuation

4.1 Lessons from an Overview of the Literature on Valuation Techniques

Tables 4.1–4.5 list some of the existing valuation studies by area of application and location, for different valuation techniques. Applications are classified as 'zero to few', 'some' and 'many', where 'some' means up to ten, and 'many' means more than ten. The list includes applications in developed and developing countries. An examination of the tables reveals several things.

First, the non-market valuation techniques described in Chapter 2 are not untested: several have been used in both industrialised and developing countries in a wide variety of sectors and areas of application.

Second, much of the valuation literature is very recent. For all the valuation techniques in all areas of application and in all parts of the world, the majority of the work has been done since 1980. This recent surge of interest in valuation work throughout the world is due to several factors. In the United States in 1981 President Ronald Reagan signed Executive Order 12291, which required that all 'major' federal regulations pass a benefit–cost test. US government agencies responsible for the management and protection of the environment and natural resources found that they needed non-market valuation techniques to estimate the benefits of regulations designed to improve environmental quality.

Perhaps even more important than Executive Order 12291 was the Comprehensive Environmental Response, Compensation, and Liability Act (CERCLA), passed by the US Congress in 1980. This legislation established that 'potentially responsible parties' could be liable for the damages caused by their spill or release of hazardous or toxic substances – to pay compensation to victims or to cover the costs of clean up. The federal and state governments were designated as the 'trustees' of the nation's natural resources and could sue corporations or individuals who damaged such resources. The US federal government was charged with developing regulations to determine how the quantum of these damages should be assessed. The regulations and procedures were slow in coming and, once promulgated, were quickly subject to legal challenge.

The most famous of the natural resources damage assessments to end up in court has been the federal and state suits against Exxon for its role in the Prince

William's Sound Oil Spill in Alaska, but there have been many other cases. The litigation process surrounding natural resource damage assessment in the United States has focused attention on the strengths and weaknesses of non-market valuation techniques in a manner largely unprecedented in 'normal' academic debate. In the Exxon-Valdez case in particular, parties to the litigation sponsored large research projects on non-market valuation in order to support or discredit the estimates of environmental damage prepared by other parties.

These two developments resulted in a period of major innovation and research in the United States during the 1980s on the theory and methods of non-market valuation. In Europe, heightened awareness of the importance of environmental issues has sparked a renewed interest in developing policy instruments that can be used to improve environmental quality. Valuation techniques are central to this effort.

As the tables show, the application of valuation techniques in Europe began even more recently than in the United States, but is now increasing rapidly. To date the majority of applications in Europe have been in Norway, Sweden, and the United Kingdom, but there is an accelerating increase in the number of applications throughout both Eastern and Western Europe. Most of the applications in developing countries are even more recent than in Europe.

Third, for all the valuation techniques the majority of applications have been carried out in the United States and Canada, the remainder being mostly in Europe. Not surprisingly, few applications have been carried out in developing countries. However, interest in valuation work is growing rapidly in Africa, Latin America and Southeast Asia as development banks and national governments seek to incorporate environmental concerns into policy and project appraisals.

Fourth, there is a surprisingly large number of applications of the contingent valuation method in comparison with those of other techniques. This is in part because the contingent valuation method is flexible in terms of data requirements and can be applied to many different kinds of valuation problem. However, there are a large number of studies in the United States using the travel cost method to estimate the value of recreational sites and activities and the value of water quality improvements. Studies using the hedonic property value method have largely focused on measuring the value of air and water quality improvements and the value of urban amenities. But most of the applications of these surrogate market methods have been made in the United States and Canada; applications in developing countries are still rare. Damage function approaches using 'dose–response' relationships and the valuation of outcomes at market or shadow prices are used more frequently in the developing world, reflecting the prevailing problems of soil erosion and deforestation.

Fifth, for all the valuation techniques the major areas of application in the United States have been air and water quality; recreation (including fishing, hunting, parks, wildlife preservation); health risks; and water supply (including groundwater protection). With a couple of exceptions, European applications have followed a similar pattern. In Europe there seems to be a greater proportion of applications in the areas of forestry and transport. In developing countries the applications have been confined to three sectors: water and sanitation; land degradation and agricultural productivity; and recreation (tourism, national parks). This is principally due to the interest and commitment of the World Bank in these areas. The same interest has now led to a marked expansion into other areas, notably air pollution and health. The growing interest in modified national income accounts has also led to an increase in the use of 'quick' valuation techniques.

Table 4.1 Numbers of studies applying the Contingent Valuation Method

Area of application	USA and Canada	Europe	Developing countries
Agriculture	Some	Few	
Air quality	Many	Many	
Climate change	Zero–few	Few	
Energy	Many	Few	Zero–few
Fishing: commercial	Some	Few	Zero–few
Fishing: recreational	Many	Few	
Forestry	Some	Many	
Health risks	Many	Many	
Recreational hunting	Many	Some	
Parks, nature reserves, & wildlife	Many	Many	Some
Roads/transport	Few	Few	
Water quality	Many	Many	Some
Water supply & sanitation (incl. groundwater protection)	Many	Some	Many

Source: Carson, R.T., N. Carson, A. Alberini, N. Flores, and J. Wright (1993); and authors' estimates.

Table 4.2 Numbers of studies applying the Travel Cost Method

Area of application	USA	Europe	Developing countries
Fishing: recreational	Many	Many	
Parks, nature reserves & wildlife	Many	Many	Some
Water quality	Many	Some	Few
Water supply, sanitation	Few	Few	

Table 4.3 Numbers of studies applying the Hedonic Property Pricing Method

Area of application	USA	Europe	Developing countries
Agriculture	Few		
Air quality	Many	Some	
Health risks	Few		
Hunting	Few		
Noise	Many	Many	
Parks, nature reserves & wildlife	Many	Some	
Water quality	Few		
Water supply & sanitation	Few	Few	Few

Table 4.4 Numbers of studies applying the Dose–Response (damage function) method

Area of application	USA	Europe	Developing countries
Agriculture	Many	Some	Many
Air quality	Many	Many	Some
Fishing: commercial		Few	Many
Health risks	Many	Some	Many*
Materials damage	Many	Many	
Water quality	Few		Few
Water supply, sanitation		Few	Few

Note: * Inclusive of the Economies in Transition.

Table 4.5 Numbers of studies applying Benefits Transfer methods

Area of application	USA	Europe	Developing countries
Forestry	Few		
Recreation	Many		
Water quality	Some		
Air quality	Few		

4.2 Choosing Valuation Techniques

All the valuation techniques have strengths and weaknesses, and the decision on which to use for a particular application requires experience and judgement on the part of the analyst. Some general points for the analyst to consider when making this choice are set out below.

First, it is often possible to use more than one valuation technique and compare the results. All methods involve some uncertainty; if the analyst has multiple estimates, he or she will have greater confidence in the value of the proposed change.

Several of the valuation techniques typically use data from a household survey (for example contingent valuation, travel cost and hedonic property pricing methods). When a technique requires that primary data be collected with a household survey, it is often possible to design the survey to obtain the data necessary to undertake more than one valuation method. This approach is particularly useful in developing countries because reliable secondary data are rarely available for carrying out valuation work. Household surveys are required for contingent valuation, opportunity cost and travel cost studies. Such surveys need to be designed with the goal of producing value estimates using multiple methods.

Second, different valuation techniques may measure different things. In this sense they should be considered as complimentary rather than competing tools. For example, the contingent valuation method is the only available technique for measuring non-use (or passive use) values. Suppose that estimates of use value of a national park and wildlife reserve were obtained using a travel cost model and estimates of non-use value were obtained from a contingent valuation survey. These value estimates are not substitutes for one another; both are useful for policy makers.

Similarly, revealed preference methods measure the perceived benefits to individuals; they do not capture the value of effects of which people are unaware. For example, if individuals do not know that a cancer-causing substance is in their drinking water, they obviously will not take action to avoid this risk. There will thus be no 'behavioural trail' that an analyst can follow to determine how much they would be willing to pay to avoid such a risk. However, using the damage function approach, an analyst could estimate the reduced cancer deaths that would result if the carcinogenic substance were to be removed from the water supply.

Third, it is important to consider the needs of the user(s) of valuation studies. In some cases clients have preferences for the use of one valuation technique over another. For example, estimates obtained from travel cost or hedonic property pricing methods may be considered too theoretical or too complex. A particular client may feel that contingent valuation estimates are too subjective and unreliable to support policy debate and discussion. The analyst carrying out policy work must be sensitive to such concerns.

Fourth, the analyst should consider not only the client's needs, but also the needs of the public. Information elicited on people's values for environmental improvement is often of great interest to a wide variety of groups in society. In choosing a valuation technique, thought should be given to how the information obtained will be received by the public and interested parties other than the immediate client. Information from valuation studies could be used in a 'top-down' hierarchical planning process or it could contribute to democratic dialogue or a participatory political process. A technique such as contingent valuation bears a resemblance to a referendum or voting process. Whereas the final decision on a policy or project may not be determined by an election, the process of eliciting information on people's preferences involves a certain degree of participation in decision making. Analysts need to be aware of the consultative nature of the valuation task and sensitive to the political implications. They should choose techniques that inform and facilitate public debate. One useful step is to hold public hearings or meetings with local community leaders to explain the findings of valuation studies.

Fifth, the cost of carrying out a valuation study or set of studies must be weighed against the value of the information in helping to make a better policy or project decision. Clearly more money could be spent on a valuation study than a policy decision warrants. But it is also important to keep in mind that many policies and projects have large scale environmental implications that extend far into the future. In this case there is a substantial risk that too little money will be spent on the use of valuation techniques.

4.3 Summary of Valuation Techniques and Their Relative Strengths

To conclude this chapter on guidance for the analyst we set out below brief summaries of the main techniques and their relative strengths and weaknesses.

4.3.1 Contingent Valuation Method (CVM)

Range of Applicability
Extensive, since it can be used to derive values for almost any environmental change. This explains its attractiveness to 'valuers'. Only method for eliciting non-use values. Successfully applied in developing countries to water supply, water quality, forest access.

Procedure
Involves administering a carefully worded questionnaire which asks people their WTP and/or WTA compensation for a specified environmental change. Econometric analysis of survey results is generally required to derive mean values of WTP bids and to estimate the determinants of respondents' WTP. Literature tends

to suggest that most sensible results come from cases where respondents are familiar with the asset being 'valued'.

Validity   The literature has identified various forms of potential bias. 'Strategic bias' arises if respondents intentionally give responses that do not reflect their 'true' values. They may do this if they think there is potential to 'free ride'. However, there is limited evidence of strategic bias. 'Hypothetical bias' arises because respondents are not making 'real' transactions. Costs of studies usually limits the number of experiments involving real money (criterion validity), but some studies exist. Convergent validity is good. Construct validity – relating value estimates to expectations of values estimated using other measures – is debated, especially the marked divergence in many studies between WTP and WTA compensation.

Reference   Case material is extensively reviewed in Mitchell, R. and Carson, R. (1989).

4.3.2 Contingent Ranking Method (CRM)

Range of   Extensive. Limited number of studies exist and are confined to
Applicability 'private goods' – that is goods purchased in the market place. It is unclear how extensive the range of application could be for environmental goods but this is under investigation in the context of house location decisions.

Procedure   Individuals are asked to rank several alternatives rather than express a WTP. Alternatives tend to differ according to some risk characteristic and price. Method could be extended to a ranking of house characteristics with some 'anchor' such as the house price being used to convert rankings into WTP.

Validity   Not widely discussed in the literature but is theoretically valid. Too few studies exist to test other validity measures but initial results suggest CRM WTP exceeds CVM WTP.

Reference   Magat, W., Viscusi, W.K. and Huber, J. (1987).

4.3.3 Conventional market approaches (including dose–reponse, replacement cost, and opportunity cost approaches)

Range of
Applicability

Extensively used where 'dose–response' relationships between pollution and output or impact are known. Examples include crop and forest damage from air pollution, materials damage, health impacts of pollution, output losses from soil erosion, sedimentation from soil erosion. Limited to cases where there are markets or where shadow prices can be estimated – that is the method cannot be used to estimate non-use values.

Replacement cost approaches also widely used because it is often relatively easy to find estimates of such costs. Replacement cost approaches should be confined to situations where the cost relates to achieving some agreed environmental standard, or where there is an overall constraint requiring that a certain level of environmental quality is achieved.

Opportunity cost approaches are very useful where a policy precludes access to an area – for example estimating forgone money and in-kind incomes from establishment of a protected area. Numerous applications in developing countries.

Procedure

Dose–response: takes physical and ecological links between pollution ('dose') and impact ('response') and values the final impact at a market or shadow price. Most of the effort usually resides in the non-economic exercise of establishing the dose–response links. Multiple regression techniques often used for this.

Replacement Cost: ascertain environmental damage and then estimate cost of restoring environment to its original state.

Opportunity Cost: ascertain functions of displaced land use and estimate in-kind and money incomes from those uses. May require detailed household surveys to establish economic and leisure activities in the area in question.

Validity

Dose–response: theoretically a sound approach. Uncertainty resides mainly in the errors in the dose–response relationship for example where, if they exist, are threshold levels before damage occurs? Are there 'jumps' (discontinuities) in the dose–damage relationship? An adequate 'pool' of studies may not be available for cross-reference.

Criterion validity not relevant since presence of 'real' markets tends to be a test in itself – that is revealed preferences in the market place are being used as the appropriate measure of value.

Replacement Cost: validity limited to contexts where agreed standards must be met.

Opportunity Cost: sound measure of damage done by a given

	land use that precludes other activity. More sophisticated estimates would include lost consumer surplus.

Expense   Dose–response can be costly if large databases need to be assembled and manipulated in order to establish dose–response relationships. If dose–response functions already exist, the method can be very inexpensive and quick. Replacement cost is inexpensive if engineering data exists.

Reference   US Environmental Protection Agency (1985).

4.3.4 Surrogate markets: avertive behaviour

Range of   Limited to cases where households spend money to offset
Applicability environmental hazards, but these can be important – for example noise insulation expenditures; risk-reducing expenditures such as smoke-detectors, safety belts, water filters, and so on Application in developing countries uncertain – probably small.

Has not been used to estimate non-use values though arguable that payments to some wildlife societies could be interpreted as insurance payments for conservation.

Procedure   Whilst used comparatively rarely, the approach is potentially important. Expenditures undertaken by households and designed to offset an environmental risk need to be identified. Examples include noise abatement, reactions to radon gas exposure – for example purchase of monitoring equipment, visits to medics, and so on

Validity   Theoretically correct. Insufficient studies to comment on convergent validity. Uses actual expenditures so criterion validity is generally met.

Expense   Econometric analysis on panel and survey data is sometimes needed. Can be fairly expensive.

Reference   Dickie, D., Gerking, S. and Agee, M. (1991).

4.3.5 Surrogate markets: travel cost method

Range of   Generally limited to site characteristics and to valuation of time.
Applicability Former tends to be recreational sites. Latter often known as discrete choice – for example implicit value of time can be estimated by observing how choice between travel modes is made or how choice of good relates to travel time avoided (last case has been used to value women's water collection time in developing countries).

Cannot be used to estimate non-use values.

Procedure   Detailed sample survey needed of travellers or households, together with their costs of travel to the site. Complications

	include other possible benefits of the travelling, and presence of competing sites.
Validity	Theoretically correct, but complicated when there are multi-purpose trips and competing sites. Some doubts about 'construct validity' in that number of trips should be inversely correlated with 'price' of trips – that is, distance travelled. Some UK studies do not show this relationship. Convergent validity generally good in US studies. Generally acceptable to official agencies and conservation groups.
Reference	Willis, K. and Benson, J. (1988).

4.3.6 Surrogate markets: hedonic property pricing

Range of Applicability	Applicable only to environmental attributes likely to be capitalised into the price of housing and/or land. Most relevant to noise and air pollution and neighbourhood amenity.
	Does not measure non-use value and is confined to cases where property owners are aware of environmental variables and act because of them (as with avertive behaviour).
Procedure	Approach generally involves assembly of cross-sectional data on house sales or house price estimates by estate agents, together with data on factors likely to influence these prices. Multiple regression techniques are then needed to obtain the first estimate of an 'implicit price'. A further stage of analysis is required since the multiple regression approach does not identify the demand curve directly.
Validity	Theoretically sound, though market failures may mean that prices are distorted, that is markets may not behave as required by the approach. Data on prices and factors determining prices often difficult to come by. Limited tests of convergent validity but generally encouraging results.
Reference	Brookshire, D. *et al.* (1982).

4.3.7 Surrogate markets: hedonic wage-risk estimation

Range of Applicability	Limited to valuation of morbidity and mortality risks in occupations. Resulting 'values of life' have been widely used and applied elsewhere, for example in the dose–response approach.
Procedure	As with other hedonic pricing methods, the approach uses multiple regression to relate wages/salaries to factors influencing them. Included in the determining factors is a measure of risk of accident. The resulting 'wage premium' can then be related to risk factors to derive the so-called value of a statistical life.
Validity	Theoretically sound. Convergent validity may be tested against

CVM of risk reduction, but wage-risk approach measures WTA compensation not WTP.

Reference   Marin, A. and Psacharopoulos, G. (1982).

REFERENCES

Brookshire, D., Thayer, M.A., Schulze, W.D. and d'Arge, R.C. (1982), 'Valuing Public Goods: A Comparison of Survey and Hedonic Approaches', *American Economic Review*, 72 (1).

Carson, R.T., Carson, N., Alberini, A., Flores, N. and Wright, J. (1993), *A Bibliography of Contingent Valuation Studies and Papers*, Draft, La Jolla, California: Natural Resource Damage Assessment Inc.

Dickie, D., Gerking, S. and Agee, M. (1991) 'Health benefits of Persistent Micropollutant Control: the Case of Stratospheric Ozone Depletion and Skin Damage Risks', in Opschoor, J.B. and Pearce, D.W. (eds), *Persistent Pollutants: Economics and Policy*, Dordrecht: Kluwer.

Magat, W., Viscusi, W.K. and Huber, J. (1987), 'Paired Comparisons and Contingent Valuation Approaches to Morbidity Risk Valuation', *Journal of Environmental Economics and Management*, 15.

Marin, A. and Psacharopoulos, G. (1982), 'The Reward for Risk in the Labour Market: Evidence from the United Kingdom and a Reconciliation with Other Studies', *Journal of Political Economy*, 90.

Mitchell, R. and Carson, R. (1989), *Using Surveys to Value Public Goods: the Contingent Valuation Method*, Washington DC: Resources for the Future.

US Environmental Protection Agency (1985), *Costs and Benefits of Reducing Lead in Gasoline: Final Regulatory Impact Analysis*, Washington DC: EPA–230–05–85–006.

Willis, K. and Benson, J. (1988), 'Valuation of Wildlife: A Case Study on the Upper Teesdale Site of Special Scientific Interest and Comparison of Methods in Environmental Economics', in Turner, R.K. (ed), *Sustainable Environmental Management: Principles and Practice*, London: Belhaven Press.

5. Problems with Applying Valuation Techniques in Developing Economies

5.1 Introduction

Chapter 4 assessed the 'state of the art' in the application of economic valuation techniques in both developed and developing economies. Probably the most significant finding is that valuation techniques are extensively applied in developing economies, despite the fact that research into and application of valuation techniques is a comparatively recent phenomenon even in developed economies. However, there are problems with applying valuation techniques that are particular to developing economies. This chapter looks some of at the remaining problem areas.

5.2 Data Problems

Valuation techniques have been applied in developing economies despite the fact that many developing economies operate with administered markets in which the price mechanism is not allowed to function fully. This explains why techniques requiring well-functioning markets – notably the hedonic property and hedonic wage techniques – are the least cited examples of valuation in the developing world (see summaries in Chapter 4). However, there is scope to apply hedonic pricing techniques in developing economies; markets in land work well in many countries. Unfortunately even when the market functions fully, records of sale prices are rarely kept in any detail, leading to serious data problems.

Data problems also exist for the 'damage function' (dose–response) technique. However, these data problems usually relate to the nature of the dose–response functions rather than the required market or shadow prices. The latter are typically crop prices, timber values, local market prices and so on, and these are either available centrally or through careful inspection of local markets, increasing the importance of field work. The opportunity cost approach also requires careful fieldwork in the form of household surveys to find out what uses households make of given land areas, for example forests.

The contingent valuation, discrete choice and travel cost techniques all require primary data collection. This perhaps explains their evident success in developing economy applications as, by and large, they avoid the use of secondary data sources.

5.3 Rapid Appraisal Versus Intensive Surveys

The analyst will quickly face a major issue in the application of valuation techniques in developing economies. If, as argued in Section 5.2, the most attractive valuation techniques are those which generate their own data, then what is the cost of such surveys? Discussion with those who have carried out survey work shows that the cost of contingent valuations has varied from under US$10,000 to over US$250,000. Given the need for careful questionnaire design, pre-testing and large sample size (1000 +), it is clear that a good contingent valuation study will cost at least US$100,000–200,000. It is also clear that few agencies will agree to spend this much. Only one or two European contingent valuation studies have cost more than US$40,000 – the vast majority have cost a few thousand. Costs can be limited by using 'cheap' survey staff (for example students), but there will be a trade-off between cost and the quality of survey results.

Wherever possible, more expensive studies are to be preferred. There are two reasons for this.

First, even at a cost of US$100,000, a contingent valuation study will account for only a fraction of a percent of the cost of the project in question and can result in improvements in project or policy design worth much more than the cost of the study. Agencies and governments are not easily persuaded of the sense of this observation, but the analyst should persist. The cost of a survey should be weighed against the social importance of the outcome. Where the livelihoods of a large number of people are at stake, expenditure on a contingent valuation study is likely to be small relative to the social importance of its findings.

Second, contingent valuation studies serve several functions. While the focus in this volume has been on the estimates of values produced, it is worth remembering that contingent valuation also reveals considerable amounts of information about what local people want. Contingent valuation can therefore be used as a vehicle for public participation in decision making. This is a factor in favour of contingent valuation, especially as we are recognising that many investments 'fail' because of a lack of consultation and assessment of local wants and needs. The high cost of a contingent valuation study therefore needs to be compared to the multiple benefits of the surveys carried out.

Ultimately, there will be a trade-off, and the issue will arise as to whether low cost, 'rapid appraisal' techniques are reliable. The analyst must judge. Criteria for judgement are likely to include reference to similar cases in the literature, as listed in Chapter 6.

5.4 Time and the Discount Rate

This volume has not been concerned with project evaluation generally, only with the issue of environmental valuation. None the less, there remain problems in project evaluation which have not been satisfactorily resolved. The main one is the choice of discount rate. This is also a 'price' or 'value' in that it signals the rate at which present and future consumption is to be traded.

The emergence of the sustainable development concept has focused attention on the discount rate. High rates reduce the 'present value' of future benefits and costs and so appear to discriminate against the future, and hence against sustainability. Low rates favour the future, but are perhaps inimical to immediate economic development.

High rates (ten percent and above, in real terms) tend to be justified by reference to the opportunity cost of capital, that is the rate of return that could be earned on a marginal project in the developing economy. However, investments tend to displace both consumption and investment, so that the relevant discount rate should be that which relates to consumption flows. The discount rate should therefore be applied to flows of benefits and costs converted to consumption units. That is, the numeraire is consumption and the discount rate is the consumption rate of interest (*CRI*). Values of the *CRI* tend to be based on the 'standard' formula:

$$CRI = a + bg \qquad (5.1)$$

where 'a' is the pure time preference rate, 'b' is the elasticity of the marginal utility of income function, and 'g' is the expected growth rate in real consumption. Values of the *CRI* are unlikely to exceed four to six percent in most developing countries. Even then, the extent to which such rates adequately account for concerns about environmental problems inherited by future generations can be questioned.

The discount rate problem remains and none of the recent developments in the literature will assist the analyst in resolving the problem in any clear-cut fashion.

5.5 Training and Environmental Economics

It is not a surprise that most valuation exercises in developing economies are carried out by experts from North America and Europe – comparatively few are led by economists from the country in which the study is carried out. This mainly reflects the state of education in environmental economics in developing economies. By and large, environmental economics is not taught in developing economy universities nor are agency and government staff trained in the subject.

There are several solutions to this situation. The first is 'in place training' whereby institutions from developed economies provide short courses within the countries in question. This is the option pursued, for example, by the United Nations University which has run training sessions in Malta, India, the West Indies and parts of Africa. One problem with this approach is that the training is effective at the time but staff quickly lose the incentive to use the training once the sessions have ended. This can only be overcome by continued involvement, probably through an actual project. Above all, commitment 'from the top' is essential.

The second solution is the release of staff to training institutions – usually universities – in developed economies. The advantage of this is that individuals gain greater exposure to training staff, meet with other trainees from different countries, and may be able to secure longer term assignments. The disadvantage is that expectations may be raised too high relative to the institutional capacity in the trainee's country. There are also risks of trainees finding opportunities to work in agencies in the developed economies, thus defeating the object of the exercise.

The reality is that those responsible for guiding decisions – usually civil servants – are not well trained in environmental economics even in most developed economies. Moreover, environmental economics as it applies to developing economies remains a subject practised by comparatively few economists. It is clear that sponsorship and encouragement of institutional capacity in both developed and developing countries is needed to increase understanding of environmental economics amongst policy makers.

6. Annotated Bibliography

This chapter lists the available case studies on valuation in developing countries. Also included are selected references to assist readers in placing the studies in their context, or which offer guidance on the problems of economic valuation. The bibliography reports only studies relevant to the monetary valuation of environmental costs and benefits in developing countries. The references are coded as follows:

C   case study involving report of empirical estimates of willingness-to-pay (WTP) or willingness-to-accept (WTA) in developing countries.
G   general
M   methodological contribution
N   national accounting exercise

No detailed manual exists (as of 1995) on the application of valuation techniques in developing countries. But useful chapters on procedures for valuation can be found in Pearce, D.W. Whittington, D. and Georgiou, S. (1994) *Project and Policy Appraisal: Integrating Economics and Environment*, Paris: OECD.

6.1 General References

6.1.1 Texts on valuation

Bentkover, J.D., Covello, V. and Mumpower, J. (1986), *Benefits Assessment: The State of the Art*, Dordrecht, Netherlands: D. Reidel Publishing Company.

Braden, J.B. and Kolstad, C.D. (1991), *Measuring the Demand for Environmental Quality*, Amsterdam: North Holland.

This is one of the most thorough and wide ranging texts on the theoretical foundations and applications of economic valuation.

Freeman, A.M. III (1979), *The Benefits of Environmental Improvement: Theory and Practice*, Baltimore: Johns Hopkins University Press.

Now dated, and superseded by:

Freeman, A.M. III (1993), *The Measurement of Environmental and Resource Values: Theory and Methods*, Washington DC: Resources for the Future.

This is perhaps the most recommended text on valuation along with Braden and Kolstad above.

Johansson, P.O. (1987), *The Economic Theory and Measurement of Environmental Benefits*, Cambridge: Cambridge University Press.

Mitchell, R.B. and Carson, R.T. (1989), *Using Surveys to Value Public Goods: The Contingent Valuation Method*, Washington DC: Resources for the Future

This is the 'classic' reference for contingent valuation.

Pearce, D.W. and Markandya, A. (1989), *The Benefits of Environmental Policy: Monetary Valuation*, Paris: OECD.

Contains brief overviews of each technique.

Pearce, D.W., Whittington, D. and Georgiou, S. (1994), *Project and Policy Appraisal: Integrating Economics and Environment*, Paris: OECD.

Contains chapters on each of the valuation techniques and pays attention to applications in both developed and developing economies.

6.1.2 General material relating to developing countries

G Barbier, E. (1993), Valuation of Environmental Resources and Impacts in Developing Countries, in Turner, R.K. (ed.), *Sustainable Environmental Economic and Management: Principles and Practice*, London: Belhaven Press, pp. 319–337.

G Bojö, J., Mäler K.G. and Unemo, L. (1992), *Environment and Development: an Economic Approach*, (revised edition), Dordrecht: Kluwer.

G Dixon, J., Carpenter, R., Fallon, L., Sherman, P. and Manipomoke, S. (1986), *Economic Analysis of the Environmental Impacts of Development Projects*, London: Earthscan Publications.

Substantially revised and extended edition:

Dixon, J., Carpenter, R., Scura, L., Sherman, P. (1994), *Economic Analysis of the Environmental Impacts*, London: Earthscan Publications.

Proposes economic valuation methodologies of the impact of development projects on the environment. Calls for the systematic evaluation of all the intentional and unintentional consequences of development initiatives.

G Dixon, J. and Hufschmidt, M. (1986), *Economic Valuation Techniques for the Environment: A Case Study Handbook*, Baltimore: The John Hopkins University Press.

The authors present detailed case studies to demonstrate application of techniques to value the environmental effects of development. A hypothetical case study illustrates important differences between market and shadow prices. Actual case studies follow.

G Dixon, J. and Sherman, P. (1990), *Economics of Protected Areas: A New Look at Benefits and Costs*, London: Earthscan Publications.

Assesses the costs and benefits associated with maintaining protected areas, and discusses methods for assigning monetary values to natural environmental assets. Specific case studies for several developing countries are also presented.

G   Dixon, J., James, D. and Sherman, P. (1990), *Dryland Management: Economic Case Studies*, London: Earthscan.

G   Evenson, R. (1991), *Valuing Environmental Benefits in Developing Economies*, Proceedings of a Seminar Series held in Feb–May 1990 at Michigan State University.

A collection of case studies reviewed individually elsewhere in this volume.

G   Hufschmidt, M., James, D., Meister, A., Bower, B. and Dixon, J. (1983), *Environment, Natural Systems, and Development: an Economic Valuation Guide*, Baltimore: Johns Hopkins University Press.

M   Mäler, K.G. (1992), *Production Function Approach in Developing Countries*, Beijer Institute Reprint Series No. 6, Stockholm, Sweden: Beijer Institute.

This paper analyses valuation problems connected with environmental resources in terms of the production function and suggests widespread applicability of the technique.

G   Munasinghe, M. (1993a), *Environmental Economics and Sustainable Development*, World Bank Environmental Department, Paper No. 3, Washington, DC: The World Bank.

The paper explains the key role played by environmental economics in facilitating the more effective incorporation of environmental concerns into development decision making. Concepts and techniques of valuation of environmental impacts and key related aspects are explicitly considered. Two case studies (Madagascar and Sri Lanka) are discussed, and a number of other case studies are summarised.

G   Munasinghe, M. (ed.) (1993b), *Environmental Economics and Natural Resource Management in Developing Countries*, Committee of International Development Institutions on the Environment (CIDIE), Washington DC: World Bank.

Collected papers on theory and application of valuation techniques in developing countries.

G   Munasinghe, M. and Lutz, E. (1993), 'Environmental Economics and Valuation in Development Decision Making' (sic), in Munasinghe (1993b),

G   Pearce, D.W., Barbier, E. and Markandya, A. (1990), *Sustainable*
C   *Development: Economics and Environment in the Third World*, London: Earthscan Publications.

The book offers a definition of sustainable development in terms of not depleting resources, and then examines its economic implications. The importance of discount rates and economic appraisal is emphasised. The bulk of the book contains six case studies of major developmental issues in the Third World.

G Pearce, D.W. and Markandya, A. (1992), 'Marginal Opportunity Cost as a Planning Concept in Natural Resource Management', in Schramm, G. and Warford, J. (ed.), *Environmental Management and Economic Development*, Baltimore: The Johns Hopkins University Press.

In the context of non-sustainable use of renewable resources, proposes Marginal Opportunity Cost functions as an organising concept. Because expectations have to be formed about future resource exploitation and the likely state of the environment in the future, estimation of MOC requires extensive information. The results are an essential tool in the planning and management of natural resources.

G Pearce, D.W. (1993), *Economic Values and the Natural World*, London: Earthscan Publications.

The book deals with how and why to attribute economic values to environmental features. Economic analyses and different methods of valuing people's preferences for environmental quality provide an economic rationale for dealing with global environmental problems. Numerous case studies are presented to illustrate the economic approaches for placing monetary values on people's preferences for environmental quality.

G Pearce, D.W and Turner, R.K. (1992), *Benefits Estimates and Environmental Decision Making*, Paris: OECD.

The book assesses the reasons why valuation methodologies are not widely used in practice. The results are based on surveys carried out in six developed countries.

G Schramm, G. and Warford, J. (eds) (1989), *Environmental Management and Economic Development*, Baltimore, USA: The Johns Hopkins University Press.

This volume shows that much environmental damage is the result of either short-sighted policies or lack of knowledge. The focus is on how developing countries can protect and improve their natural environment while simultaneously improving the welfare of their people. Environmental protection and economic development do not necessarily stand as opposed choices. Rather they often go hand in hand. The authors look at the analytical and methodological questions, illustrate many of the problems, and point to possible solutions.

C Spurgeon, J. and Alyward, B. (1992), *The Economic Value of Ecosystems: Coral Reefs*, London Environmental Economics Centre Gatekeeper Series 92–03, London: International Institute for Environment and Development.

G Winpenny, J. (1991), *Values for the Environment: A Guide to Economic Appraisal*, London: Her Majesty's Stationery Office.

Aimed at economists and practitioners, this practical guide to the economic treatment of the environment in project appraisal uses cost–benefit analysis as the decision framework.

6.2 Biodiversity (see also Wetlands, Forest Functions)

M Artuso, A. (1994), *Economic Analysis of Biodiversity as a Source of Pharmaceuticals*, Paper for the PAHO/IICA Conference on Biodiversity, Biotechnology and Sustainable Development, San Jose, Costa Rica.

An overview of the economic value of pharmaceuticals based on biodiversity, and an assessment of the various contractual arrangements for exploiting this value.

G Alyward, B. (1991), *The Economic Value of Ecosystems: Biological Diversity*, Gatekeeper Series 91–03, London Environmental Economics Centre, London: International Institute for Environment and Development.

G Alyward, B. and Barbier, E. (1992), *What is Biodiversity Worth to a Developing Country? Capturing the Pharmaceutical Value of Species Information*, Discussion Paper 92–05, London Environmental Economics Centre, London: International Institute for Environment and Development.

G Aylward, B. and Barbier, E. (1991), *Valuing Environmental Functions in Developing Countries: Biodiversity and Conservation*, London Environmental Economics Centre, London: International Institute for Environment and Development.

The authors detail the challenge presented by valuing environmental functions to ecologists and economists and synthesises the methodological advances that have occurred. Using tropical forests, wetlands and biodiversity as illustrations, the application of this methodology to valuing the functions of complex natural systems is investigated and existing studies reviewed.

C Aylward, B. (1993), *The Economic Value of Pharmaceutical Prospecting and Its Role in Biodiversity Conservation*, Discussion Paper 93–05, London, London Environmental Economics Centre, London: International Institute for Environment and Development.

Reveals large negative returns to biodiversity conservation for the provision of biotic samples only, using Costa Rica case study.

M Aylward, B., Echeverria J., Fendt, L. and Barbier, E. (1993), *The Economic Value of Species Information and Its Role in Biodiversity Conservation: Costa Rica's National Biodiversity Institute*, Discussion Paper 93–06, London Environmental Economics Centre, London: International Institute for Environment and Development.

Develops a framework for analysing the economic value of

biodiversity as a source of information for pharmaceutical companies.

G Barbier, E., Burgess, J. and Folke, C. (1994), *Paradise Lost? The Ecological Economics of Biodiversity*, London: Earthscan Publications.

General text on economics of biodiversity, with separate chapters on rangelands, forests, wetlands and marine systems.

G Barbier, E., Burgess, J., Swanson, T. and Pearce, D.W. (1990), *Elephants, Economics and Ivory*, London: Earthscan Publications.

The authors develop a database on the ivory trade, analyse the trade in terms of the determinants of demand and supply, and recommend a controlled trade as one of the means of ensuring future survival of the African elephant.

C Barnes, J. (forthcoming), *Economics of Wildlife Utilisation in Botswana*, Ph.D., University College London.

Analyses rate of return to various land uses including wildlife tourism, hunting, crocodile and ostrich farming in Botswana. Cattle ranching is shown to have very low rates of return.

C Brown, G. and Henry, W. (1989), *The Economic Value of Elephants*, Discussion Paper 89–12, London Environmental Economic Centre, London: International Institute for Environment and Development.

Estimates WTP of visitors to East Africa game parks to ensure seeing elephants.

C Brown, G., Swanson, T., Ward, M., and Moran, D. (1994), *Optimally Pricing Games Parks in Kenya*, Centre for Social and Economic Research on the Global Environment, University College London, *mimeograph*.

Using travel cost method and contingent valuation to estimate demand for parks and reserves in Kenya. Consumer surplus ranged from $77–134 per day using the travel cost approach, and $52–86 per day on the contingent valuation approach. The entry charge which maximises park/reserve revenues is some $43–64 more than existing charges.

G Brown, K. (1994), 'Approaches to Valuing Plant Medicines: the
M Economics of Culture or the Culture of Economics?', *Biodiversity and Conservation*, **3**, 734–750.

Argues that economic valuation approaches to plant medicines do not account for belief systems in the causes of disease and healing strategies.

M Chambers, C., Chambers, P. and Whitehead, J. (1994), 'Conservation Organisations and the Option Value to Preserve: an Application to Debt-for-Nature Swaps', *Ecological Economics*, **9**, 135–143.

Develops a theoretical model to show how option value and debt-for-nature swaps are linked, and carries out simulations to see what major influences on WTP by conservation organisations are likely to be. Indications are that 'swaps' are likely to be more attractive in the future.

C   Dixon, J. (1993), 'Meeting Ecological and Economic Goals: Marine Parks in the Caribbean', *Ambio*, **22**, 2–3.

The paper examines issues of protection of endangered marine ecosystems and the biodiversity they support, and the trade-offs that exist between protection and use in the context of Caribbean marine parks. Initial results indicate that proper management can yield both protection and development benefits but questions of ecosystem carrying capacity and national retention of revenues raises important issues for longer term sustainability.

C   Dixon, J., Fallon Scura, L. and van't Hof, T. (1995), 'Ecology and Microeconomics of Joint Products: the Bonaire Marine Park in the Caribbean', in Perrings, C., Maler, K.G., Folke, C., Holling, C. and Jansson B.O. (eds), *Biodiversity Conservation*, Dordrecht: Kluwer, pp. 127–146.

The 'joint production' of tourism and conservation in Bonaire is explored. The focus is on the financial returns from world class diving: gross revenues to the island's private sector, and user fees in the marine park. The resulting revenues (around $23 million a year) greatly exceed the direct costs of protection, but the opportunity costs of protection could not be estimated.

C   Echeverría, J., Hanrahan, M. and Solórzano, R. (1995), 'Valuation of Non-priced Amenities Provided by the Biological Resources Within the Moneteverde Cloud Forest Preserve, Costa Rica', *Ecological Economics*, **13**, 43–52.

A CVM was conducted to assess WTP of visitors to Monteverde to prevent conversion to agriculture. Significant findings are: total WTP ($37.5 m) greatly exceeded the conversion value; and average WTP of Costa Ricans actually exceeded that of non-Costa Ricans by 15 percent even though the incomes of the latter are nearly three times higher.

C   Hadker. N., Sharma, S., David, A., Muraleedharan T.R., Geetha, S. and Babu, P. (1995), *Are People in Developing Countries Willing to Pay for Natural Reserve Preservation?: Evidence from a CV of the Borivli National Park, Bombay*, Discussion Paper 121, Bombay: Indira Gandhi Institute of Development Research.

The Borivli National park has come under financial pressure and the authors investigate the WTP to maintain it, using a CVM approach. Annual WTP of Bombay residents amounted to some 266 million rupees, substantially in excess of current annual maintenance expenditures.

M   Hanley, N., Spash, C. and Walker, L. (1995), 'Problems in Valuing the Benefits of Biodiversity Protection', *Environmental and Resource Economics*, **5**, 249–272.

Investigates relationship of ignorance and information in the valuation of biodiversity benefits.

G   Mäler, K.G. (1993), 'The Economics of Biodiversity Loss', in Sandlund, O. and Schei, P. (eds), *Norway/UNEP Expert Conference on Biodiversity*, Hosted by the Norwegian Ministry of Environment and UNEP.

C   Mendelsohn, R. and Balick, R. (1995), 'The Value of undiscovered
M   Pharmaceuticals in Tropical Forests', *Economic Botany*, **49** (2), 223–228.

Contrary to some modern research, the authors of this paper suggest that the economic value of potential pharmaceuticals in tropical forests is very large, even if their estimate is lower than some others in circulation. They estimate net revenues to a pharmaceutical company to be $2.8 to $4.1 billion, allowing for ability to screen genetic material, likely number of undiscovered drugs, and taxation. For society as a whole, the values are higher at about $147 billion.

C   Menkhaus, S. (1993), *Measurement of Economic and Other Benefits of Wildlife Preservation: a Case Study of Keoladeo National Park, Bharatpur, India*, Institute of Economic Growth, Delhi: Delhi University, mimeograph. See also Murty, M.N. and Menkhaus, S. (1994), *Economic Aspects of Wildlife Protection in the Developing Countries: a Case Study of Keoladeo National Park, Bharatpur, India*, Paper No. E/163/94, Institute of Economic Growth, Delhi: Delhi University.

Uses contingent valuation and travel cost to assess benefits of protecting wildlife in a national park in India. While benefits exceed costs, the gainers tend to be higher income groups and the losers the low income groups. With adjustments for income utilities, the net social gains from conservation are shown to be negative. The focus is then on ways in which economic value can be captured to compensate low income groups.

G   McNeely, J. (1988), *Economics and Biological Diversity*, Gland, Switzerland: International Union for Conservation of Nature and Natural Resources.

This book focuses on sustainable forms of economic development to contribute positively to the conservation of biological diversity and the more fundamental issue of the distribution of benefits from the optimal utilisation of biological resources.

C   Moran, D. (1994), 'Contingent Valuation and Biodiversity: Measuring The User Surplus of Kenyan Protected Areas', *Biodiversity and*

Conservation, 3.

Using a contingent valuation survey, estimates non-use values for Kenyan protected areas at $450m a year, around twice the estimated opportunity costs of the conservation of these areas. Other use values would need to be added to this non-use value total.

G   Munasinghe, M. (1993), 'Environmental Economics and Biodiversity Management in Developing Countries', *Ambio*, **22** (2–3),

Environmental economics and valuation can play a key role in helping to incorporate concerns about biodiversity loss into the traditional decision making framework. A case study from Madagascar examines the impact of a new national park on tropical forests by using both conventional and newer techniques. A Sri Lankan study presents an energy–environmental analysis to eliminate projects with unacceptable impacts and to help redesign others.

G   Munasinghe, M. (1992), 'Biodiversity Protection Policy: Environmental valuation and Distribution Issues', *Ambio*, **21** (3), 227–236.

C   Narain, U. and Fisher, A.C. (1995), 'Modelling the Value of Biodiversity Using a Production Function Approach: the Case of the Anolis Lizard in the Lesser and Greater Antilles', in Perrings, C., Maler, K.G., Folke, C., Holling C. and Jansson B.O. (eds), *Biodiversity Conservation*, Dordrecht: Kluwer, pp. 115–126.

The Anolis Lizard eats pests which harm sugarcane, bananas and cocoa, thus reducing the need for pesticides. Production functions for these crops are established with and without the 'input' of the lizard. The resulting value of output due to the lizard in Trinidad and Tobago is put at $676,000 a year for a one percent reduction in the lizard population but could be $67 million for a 50 percent reduction in the lizard population.

C   Navrud, S. and Mungatana, E.D. (1994), 'Environmental Valuation in Developing Countries: The Recreational value of Wildlife Viewing', *Ecological Economics*, **11**, 135–151.

Estimates recreational value of wildlife viewing at Lake Nakuru, Kenya using CVM and TCM approaches. Annual value estimated at $7–15 million a year, with flamingos accounting for about one third of this value.

C   Norton-Griffiths, M. and Southey, C. (1995), 'The Opportunity Costs of Biodiversity Conservation in Kenya', *Ecological Economics*, **12**, 125–139.

Estimates agricultural value of Kenyan parks, reserves and forests at some $200m a year in net terms, compared to net revenues of $40 million from forestry and wildlife tourism. Suggests a strategy for reducing Kenya's contribution to this burden.

G   Pearce, D.W. (1993), 'The Economy – Biodiversity Interface' in Sandlund, O. and Schei, P. (eds), *Norway/UNEP Expert Conference on Biodiversity*, Hosted by the Norwegian Ministry of Environment and UNEP.

The paper discusses the fundamental forces underlying biodiversity loss. The central issues are rising population, assignment of property rights, market failure, intervention failure, and global appropriation failure. Also discusses ways to get around these problems with a special emphasis on creating global environmental markets.

G   Pearce, D.W. and Puroshothaman, S. (forthcoming), 'Protecting Biological Diversity: the Economic Value of Pharmaceutical Plants', in Swanson, T. (ed.), *Intellectual Property Rights and Biodiversity Conservation*, Cambridge: Cambridge University Press.

The authors examine the global commercial value of medicinal plants and calculate the likely value of one hectare of representative land for medicinal plants. If this value could be captured and appropriated, it would provide some incentive to conserve plant habitats, and prevent unsustainable exploitation and loss of global biodiversity.

G   Pearce, D.W. and Moran, D. (1994), *The Economic Value of Biological Diversity*, London: Earthscan Publications.

Expanded version of a report to the International Union for the Conservation of Nature. This book is concerned with two fundamental characteristics of the process of comparing economic values of sustainable use of biodiversity and the value of alternative resource use that threatens biodiversity: demonstration of values not reflected in the market process and realisation of those values through changes in institutional design and behaviour. The divergence between the social and private costs and benefits of biodiversity, and government and market failure explain why it is being eroded.

G   Perrings, C., Folke, C. and Mäler, K.G. (1992), *The Ecology and Economics of Biodiversity Loss: The Research Agenda*, Beijer Reprint Series No. 8, Stockholm, Sweden: Beijer Institute.

Combining the insights from the disciplines of economics and ecology, this paper outlines the most urgent questions for research in the area of biodiversity loss. The nature of the linkage between ecological and economic systems is discussed in the context of informational, institutional, ethical and cultural conditions. The paper emphasises the interdisciplinary approach to biodiversity and the gains from collaborative research.

M   Polasky, S. and Solow, A. (1993), *Measuring Biological Diversity*, Harvard Discussion Papers, mimeograph.

Shows how biological diversity can be measured in terms of

'genetic distance' between species, and how such a measure of diversity can be related to the incremental probability of discovering commercially valuable compounds.

M   Reid, W., Laird, S., Meyer, C., Gàmez, R., Sittenfeld, A., Janzen, D., Gollin, M. and Juma, C. (1993), *Biodiversity Prospecting*, USA: World Resources Institute.

The essays in this book explore the strands of thought and theory that come together in the new industry – biodiversity prospecting. Although this 'gene-rush' could damage ecosystems and the people that live in or near them, bio-prospecting can secure economic and conservation goals while underpinning the medical and agricultural advances needed to combat disease and sustain growing populations. The central concern of the book is how to manage the process correctly.

M   Simpson, R.D., Sedjo, R. and Reid, J. (1994), *Valuing Biodiversity: an Application to Genetic Prospecting*, Paper 94–20, Washington DC: Resources for the Future.

Argues that the 'genetic value' of the marginal hectare of the marginal species is likely to be insignificant and hence the benefits of genetic prospecting as a basis for conserving habitat should not be exaggerated.

M   Solow, A., Polasky, S. and Broadus, J. (1993), 'On the Measurement of Biological Diversity', *Journal of Environmental Economics and Management*, **24**, 60–68.

Develops measures of biodiversity based on genetic distance.

M   Weitzman, M. (1992), 'On Diversity', *Quarterly Journal of Economics*, **CVII**, 363–406.

Original source for practical measurement of diversity in terms of genetic distance.

M   Weitzman, M. (1993), 'What to Preserve ? An Application of Diversity Theory to Crane Conservation', *Quarterly Journal of Economics*, **CVIII**, 157–184.

6.3 Climate Change

Only research reporting damage estimates to developing countries.

C   Ayres, R. and Walter, J. (1991), 'The Greenhouse Effect: Damages, Costs and Abatement', *Environmental and Resource Economics*, **1** (3), 237–270.

Includes some estimates of costs of refugees displaced by sea level rise and famine.

C   Fankhauser, S. (1993), 'Global Warming Damage Costs: Some Monetary
    Estimates', in Kaya, Y., Nakicenovic, N., Nordhaus, W. and Toth, F.
    (eds), *Costs, Impacts and Benefits of CO_2 Mitigation*, CP 93–2,
    Laxenberg, Austria: International Institute for Applied Systems Analysis,
    pp. 85–106.
      Includes estimates for refugees but notes that presence of coastal
    protection schemes will keep numbers of refugees down.
    Fankhauser, S. (1995), *Valuing Climate Change: The Economics of the
    Greenhouse*, London: Earthscan Publications.
      Includes world regional breakdown of damages and shows, for example,
    that damage costs in China could be 3–4 times those of the rich world
    when expressed as a percentage of GNP.
C   Milliman, J.D., Broadus, J. and Gable, F. (1989), 'Environmental and
    Economic Implications of Rising Sea Level and Subsiding Deltas: The
    Nile and Bengal Examples', *Ambio*, 18 (6), 340–345.
C   Asian Development Bank (1994), *Climate Change in Asia: Eight Country
    Studies*, Manila: Asian Development Bank.
      Reports estimates of economic value of damages to various countries in
    Asia from global warming. Sea level rise alone might give rise to losses
    equal to 5 percent of GNP in Bangladesh; 1 percent in India; relocation of
    some 800,000 households in Indonesia at a cost of some $8 billion, and
    marked health impacts from increased malaria, diarrhoea and dengue
    fever, and so on.
C   Pearce D.W., Cline, W., Achanta, A., Fankhauser, S., Pachauri, R., Tol, R.
    and Vellinga, P. (1995), *The Social Costs of Climate Change:
    Greenhouse Damages and the Benefits of Control*, Chapter 6 of
    Intergovernmental Panel on Climate Change, IPCC Working Group III.
      Summarises available economic impact studies including those covering
    developing countries.

6.4   Coastal Areas

C   Bennett, E. and Reynolds, C. (1993), 'The Value of Mangrove Area in
    Sarawak', *Biodiversity and Conservation*, 2, 359–375.
      Estimates economic value of marine fisheries in Sarawak Mangroves
    Forest Area at $21 million a year, timber products at $0.12 million a year,
    and tourism at $3.7 million a year. Threats to the area include aquaculture
    ponds and palm plantations. Loss of the mangrove would also necessitate
    extensive engineering works to prevent flooding, and so on.
C   Ruitenbeek, H.J. (1994), 'Modelling Economy–Ecology Linkages in
    Mangroves: Economic Evidence for Promoting Conservation in Bintuni
    Bay, Sarawak', *Ecological Economics*, 10, 233–247.
      Presents a strong economic case for conservation of mangroves against

threats of exploitation for woodchip exports. Traditional non-commercial uses of the mangrove are estimated to be worth $10 million a year for Bintuni Bay; commercial fisheries at $35 million; and selective mangrove cutting at $20 million a year. Sustainable cutting of 25 percent of the harvestable mangrove is estimated to be worth $35 million more in present value terms than the alternative of clear-cutting.

6.5   Discount Rates

C   Cuesta, M., Carlson, G. and Lutz, E. (1994), *An Empirical Assessment of Farmers' Discount Rates in Costa Rica and Its Implication for Soil Conservation*, Environment Department, World Bank, mimeograph.

Represents the only rigorous attempt to date to measure individuals' discount rates in a developing country. Uses contingent valuation of farmers who were asked if they would invest in an investment yielding Q+r given an initial endowment of income Q, where the time horizon also varies. Results suggest that the discount rate is around 18.5 percent (real) on average; with a spread covering 95 percent of farmers equal to 15–22 percent. Actual market rates are embraced by these estimates.

6.6   Forest Function (for mangroves see coastal areas)

C   Ahmad, N. (1993), 'The Rural Development and Environmental Protection Project in the Day Forest in Djibouti: a Case Study', in Munasinghe, M. (ed.) (1993b), *Environmental Economics and Natural Resource Management in Developing Countries*, Committee of International Development Institutions on the Environment (CIDIE), Washington DC: World Bank.

Evaluates benefits of a forest in terms of wood, forage and charcoal production.

C   Anderson, D. (1987), *The Economics of Afforestation: A Case Study in Africa*, World Bank Occasional Paper No. 1 New Series, Washington DC: World Bank.

Evaluates the benefits of afforestation in terms of fuelwood and fodder supply, wind protection and impacts on crops generally. Shows that high economic rates of return can be expected from agro-forestry and windbreaks when full benefits are accounted for.

C   Anderson, D. (1989), 'Economic Aspects of Afforestation and Soil Conservation Projects', in Schramm, G. and Warford, J. (ed.) *Environmental Management and Economic Development*, Baltimore, USA: The Johns Hopkins University Press.

Presents a simple approach to estimating the economic benefits of afforestation and soil conservation projects in farming areas. Summarises

Anderson (1987).

Appasamy, P.P. (1993), 'Role of Non-timber Forest Products in a Subsistence Economy: The Case of a Joint Forestry Project in India', *Economic Botany*, **47** (3), July–September.

C   Balick, M. and Mendelsohn, R. (1992), 'Assessing the Economic Value of Traditional Medicine from Tropical Rainforests', *Conservation Biology*, **6**.

G   Barbier, E., Burgess, J., Alyward, B. and Bishop, J. (1991), *Timber Trade, Trade Policies and Environmental Degradation*, London Environmental Economics Centre Discussion Paper 92–01, London: International Institute for Environment and Development.

G   Barbier, E., Bishop, J., Alyward, B. and Burgess, J. (1992), *The Economics of Tropical Forests Land Use Options Methodology and Valuation Techniques*, London Environmental Economics Centre, London: International Institute for Environment and Development.

C   Barbier, E. (1992), 'Rehabilitating Gum Arabic Systems in Sudan: Economic and Environmental Implications', *Environmental and Resource Economics*, **2**.

   The paper explores the issues of gum arabic management in the Sudan through a crop profitability analysis of gum and other crops combined with financial and economic analysis of six representative gum arabic production systems. Only if many other factors can be maintained, will essential investments by farmers in cultivating gum be viable. The gum comes from *Acacia senegal*, an environmentally important tree in the Sahelian zone.

C   Bojö, J. (1993), 'Economic Valuation of Indigenous Woodlands', in Bradley, P.N. and McNamara, K. (eds) (1993), *Living with Trees: 'Policies for Forestry Management in Zimbabwe*, Technical Paper No. 210, Washington DC: World Bank.

   Analyses market imperfections relating to indigenous woodlands in Zimbabwe. Despite serious data problems, the paper suggests that only significant international transfers can reduce the rate of loss of Zimbabwe's woodlands due to the immediate imperative of rapid population growth.

C   Brown, K. and Pearce, D.W. (1994), 'The Economic Value of Non-Market Benefits of Tropical Forests Carbon Storage', in Weiss, S. (ed.), *The Economics of Project Appraisal and the Environment*, London: Edward Elgar.

   The paper reports estimates of economic values of carbon storage with special reference to the Amazon rainforest, and shows how carbon credits and debits affect decisions to invest in developmental land uses. The value of tropical forests as carbon stores is seen to be substantial relative to land values for agriculture.

M   Carson, R. (1995), *Valuation of Tropical Rainforests: Philosophical and Practical Issues in the Use of Contingent Valuation*, Department of Economics Discussion Paper 95–04, San Diego: University of California.

Addresses issues of how to ensure that CVM is validly used for 'global' valuations of assets such as tropical forests.

Chopra, K. (1993), 'The Value of Non-timber Forest Products: an Estimation for Tropical Deciduous Forests in India', *Economic Botany*, **47** (3), July–September.

C   Convery, F. and Tutu K. (1993), 'Estimating Gross Costs of Environmental Degradation – Sectoral Analysis: a Ghana Case Study', Ch.8 of Convery, F. (ed.), *Applying Environmental Economics in Africa*, World Bank Technical Paper No. 277, Washington DC: World Bank.

Estimates cost of forest loss due to clearance, mainly through burning, in Ghana using market price approach. Timber losses are put at $33 million a year.

C   Current, D., Lutz, E. and Scherr S. (eds) (1993), *Economic and Institutional Analysis of Agroforestry Projects in Central America and the Caribbean*, Washington DC: World Bank, mimeograph.

Collation and analysis of performance of agroforestry projects in Central America and the Caribbean. Shows estimates of benefits of such schemes in terms of wood products, manure, soil conservation, and so on.

Godoy, R., Lubowski R. and Markandya A. (1993), 'A Method for the Economic Valuation of Non-timber Tropical Forest Products', *Economic Botany*, **47** (3), July–September.

Ganesan, B. (1993), 'Extraction of Non-timber Forest Products, Including Fodder and Fuelwood, in Mudumalai, India', *Economic Botany*, **47** (3), July–September.

C   Grimes, A., Loomis, S., Jahnige, P., Burham, M., Onthank, K., Alarcón, W., Cerón, C., Neill, D., Balick, M., Bennett, B. and Mendelsohn, R. (1994), 'Valuing the Rain Forest: The Economic Value of Non-Timber Forest Products in Ecuador', *Ambio*, **23** (7), 405–410.

Through ethnobotanical and market surveys, the annual harvest levels, market prices and extraction costs of seven fruits, three medicinal barks and one resin in the Upper Napo Region of the Amazonian Ecuador are measured. The present value of net revenue from the non-timber forest products is about $1,257–$2,830, which is significantly higher than the returns from alternative land use in this area.

C   Gutman, P. (1992), *Venezuela Natural Resources Management Project, National Parks: Costs and Benefits of the Project*, Washington DC: World Bank.

Sanatilake, H.M., Senaratne D. and Abeygunawardena P. (1993), 'Role of Non-timber Forest Products in the Economy of Peripheral Communities of Knuckles National Wilderness Area of Sri Lanka', *Economic Botany*, **47** (3), July–September.

Gunatilleke, I., Gunatilleke, C. and Abeygunawardena, P. (1993), 'Interdisciplinary Research Towards Management of Non-timber Forest Resources in Lowland Rain Forests in Sri Lanka', *Economic Botany*, **47** (3), July–September.

M Hartwick, J.M. (1993), 'Forestry Economics, Deforestation, and National Accounting', in Lutz, E. (ed.) *Toward Improved Accounting for the Environment*, Washington DC: World Bank.

C Hosier, R. and Bernstein, M. (1989), *Woodfuel Use and Sustainable Development in Haiti*. Centre for Energy and the Environment, University of Pennsylvania.

Looks at Haiti's energy sector to see how its environmental problems can be reduced. Analysis shows that what is needed is simultaneous investments in enhanced woodfuel supplies, improved energy efficiency, and improved management of existing energy resources.

C Kishor, N. and Constantino, L. (1993a), *Forest Management and Competing Land Uses: an Economic Analysis for Costa Rica*, Latin America Environment Division, Washington DC: World Bank.

Although primarily concerned with an explanation for deforestation in Costa Rica, this paper estimates the value of sustainably managed forests compared to the value of cattle ranching and plantation forestry. Since sustainable forestry is found to be privately unprofitable, the environmental values are very important. These are estimated to be high at around $1,200–2,500 per hectare, with carbon sequestration dominating.

C Kishor, N and Constantino, L. (1993b), *The Costs and Benefits of Removing Log Export Bans: Evidence from Two Countries*, Latin America Environment Department, Washington DC: World Bank.

Using case studies of Canada and Costa Rica, the authors provide some preliminary estimates of the costs and benefits of removing log export bans. Benefits are about $20 million a year in Cost Rica and $180 million a year in Canada. The environmental costs could be significant, but can be offset with careful policies.

C Kramer, R., Munasinghe, M., Sharma, N., Mercer, E. and Shyamsundar, P. (1992), *Valuing a Protected Tropical Forest: A Case Study in Madagascar*. Prepared for IVth World Congress on National Parks and Protected Areas, Caracas, Venezuela, Centre for Resource and Environmental Policy, Durham, North Carolina: Duke University.

The authors highlight the importance of economic analysis in making difficult decisions regarding development versus conservation. They focus on Madagascar because of its economic poverty but genetic mega-diversity. The severe loss of species endemism has initiated a lot of concern from the government of Madagascar as well as the international community to control forest degradation and protect biodiversity.

C   Kramer, R., Mercer E. and Sharma N. (1995), *Valuing Tropical Rain Forest Protection Using the Contingent Valuation Method*, Durham, North Carolina: Duke University School of the Environment, mimeograph.

So far (1995) the only attempt to measure WTP of developed country individuals for conservation of tropical rainforests. A mail survey of US residents revealed a WTP of about $30 per household as a one-time payment to conserve 5 percent of the world's tropical forests. Across all households this would imply a total WTP of $2.7 billion.

C   Kumari, K. (1994), *Sustainable Forest Management in Malaysia*, Ph.D. Thesis, University of East Anglia, Norwich, UK.

Estimates conservation values of tropical forests in Malaysia at $1,000 a hectare, carbon storage at $2,400 a hectare, non-timber products at $100–500, ecotourism and recreation at $13–35, and pharmaceuticals at $1–100.

G   Lampietti J. and Dixon, J. (1995), *To See the Forest for the Trees: A Guide to Non-Timber Forest Benefits*, Washington DC: World Bank Environment Department, mimeograph.

Reviews the literature and suggests that timber and non-timber values account for 50 percent each of developing country forest values, compared to 33 percent and 67 percent respectively in a developed country. This excludes carbon store values. Suggests a strong policy implication that non-timber benefits are as at least important as timber benefits in forest policy.

C   Lutz, E. *et al.* (1993), *Interdisciplinary Fact Finding on Current Deforestation in Costa Rica*, Environment Department Working Paper No. 61, Washington DC: World Bank,.

C   Lynam, T., Vermeulen, S. and Campbell, B. (1991), *Contingent Valuation of Multipurpose Tree Resources in the Smallholder Farming Sector, Zimbabwe*, Paper presented to AFSRE Symposium, October.

C   Maille, P. and Mendelsohn R. (1994), 'Valuing Ecotourism in Madagascar', *Journal of Environmental Management*, **38**.

C   Mercer, E., Kramer, R. and Sharma, N. (1993), *Estimating the Nature Tourism Benefits of Establishing the Mantadia National Park in Madagascar*, Centre for Resource and Environmental Policy Research, Durham, North Carolina: Duke University.

See study by Kramer *et al.* in Chapter 4.

C   Newcombe, K. (1989), 'An Economic Justification for Rural Afforestation: The Case of Ethiopia', in Schramm, G. and Warford, J. (eds), *Environmental Management and Economic Development*, Baltimore, USA: The Johns Hopkins University Press.

Dung and crop residue have alternative value as fertiliser and soil conditioner; retaining these uses and providing agroforestry programmes is then a highly attractive, long-term strategy for supplying household fuelwood, yet increasing agricultural output. Economic value of animal dung is estimated by various means: as fuelwood substitute at market prices, and as fertiliser equivalent, showing optimal farmer strategy is to 'sell' dung on the market.

G Panayotou, T. and Ashton, P. (1992), *Not By Timber Alone: Economics and Ecology of Sustaining Tropical Forests*, Washington, DC: Island Press.

Overview of the economics of tropical forest conservation, including reference to the economic values of forest use and 'global market' value.

C Pearce, D.W. (1990), 'An Economic Approach to Saving the Tropical Forests', in Helm, D. (ed.), *Economic Policy Towards the Environment*. London: Blackwell.

The concept of total economic value offers a comprehensive framework within which to value tropical forests. There is some evidence that use values alone favour forest conservation. Existence values are at least $8 per adult in the advanced economies which could readily amount to $3 billion, or a quarter of the entire GDP contribution of classic Amazonia to Brazil's GDP, inclusive of mineral extraction, timber, and agriculture.

C Pearce, D.W. (1991), 'Deforesting the Amazon: Toward an Economic Solution', *Ecodecision*.

C Pearce, D.W. (1994), *Global Environmental Value and the Tropical Forests: Demonstration and Capture*, Centre for Social and Economic Research on the Global Environment, University College London, mimeograph.

Argues that economic values of tropical forest conservation are dominated by carbon storage values and existence values, with sustainable use values being relatively unimportant.

C Pearce, D.W., Adger, N., Brown, K., Cervigni, R. and Moran, D. (1993), *Mexico Forestry and Conservation Sector Review Substudy of Economic Valuation of Forests*. Report prepared by Centre for Social and Economic Research on the Global Environment, University of East Anglia and University College London to World Bank Latin America and the Caribbean Country Department II (LA2).

The study identifies and quantifies in monetary terms the environmental values associated with forest conservation and management. These values are typically not captured by private decision makers due to the lack of property rights in many of the forests' functions and are not considered in their production decisions. The study concludes that efforts should be made through institutions to capture global benefits.

C Peters, C., Gentry, A. and Mendelsohn, R. (1989), 'Valuation of an Amazonian Rainforest', *Nature*, **339**.

The authors argue that tropical forests can generate substantial market benefits if the appropriate resources are managed and exploited properly.

Exploiting non-wood resources while conserving the Amazon forests could prove profitable.

G   Peters, C. (1991), *Environmental Assessment of Extractive Reserves: Key*
M   *Issues in the Ecology and Management of Non-timber Forest Resources*, Institute of Economic Botany, New York: New York Botanical Garden, mimeograph.

Extensive assessment of the availability and management problems of non-timber forest products.

C   Pinedo-Vasquez, M., Zarin, D. and Jipp, P. (1992), 'Economic Returns from Forest Conversion in the Peruvian Amazon', *Ecological Economics*, 6.

The economics of timber extraction, swidden agriculture, and the harvesting of fruits and latex from the intact forest are examined and compared within a single village near Iquitos. The analysis indicates that rural populations in the area can be expected to continue converting forested land to swidden agriculture unless alternative land uses become more attractive economically.

C   Ruitenbeek, H.J. (1990a), *Evaluating Economic Policies for Promoting Rainforest Conservation in Developing Countries*, Ph.D. Thesis, London School of Economics. See Ruitenbeek (1992a).

C   Ruitenbeek, H.J. (1990b), *Economic Analysis of Tropical Forest Conservation Initiatives: Examples from West Africa*, Godalming, UK: World Wide Fund for Nature. See Ruitenbeek (1992).

C   Ruitenbeek, H.J. (1992), 'The Rainforest Supply Price: A Tool for Evaluating the Rainforest Conservation Expenditures', *Ecological Economics*, 6.

To help decide whether international resources should be used to protect specific rainforests, the calculation of a rainforest supply price is proposed. A cost–benefit analysis of a conservation project to protect Korup from increased land use suggests that it is not in Cameroon's interest unless a 5.4 million ECU inducement is transferred to Cameroon, equivalent to 1,060 ECU per km^2 per year; inducements that are within the range that conservation interests are apparently willing to mobilise.

C   Shyamsundar, P. and Kramer, R. (1993), *Does Contingent Valuation Work in Non-Market Economies?*, Centre for Resource and Environmental Policy Research, Durham, North Carolina: Duke University.

Uses contingent valuation to assess householders' preferences for access to a forest area in Madagascar.

C   Shyamsundar, P., Kramer R. and Sharma, N. (1993), *Estimating the Costs to Local Inhabitants of Establishing the Mantadia National Park in Madagascar*, Centre for Resource and Environmental Policy Research, Durham, North Carolina: Duke University.

C   Tobias, D. and Mendelsohn, R. (1991), 'Valuing Ecotourism in a Tropical Rain-Forest Reserve', *Ambio*, 20.

Using the travel cost method, the study estimates the value of ecotourism in a Costa-Rican rainforest site. The study reveals that the present value of the site per hectare based on domestic and foreign use alone is 1–2 times greater than the purchase price currently paid by the reserve for acquisition of new lands. This value does not include other potential preservation benefits like the harvesting of commodities, watershed protection, and protection of wildlife habitat and rare species.

C   World Bank (1992), *Costa Rica: Forestry Sector Review*, World Bank Report, Washington DC: World Bank.

C   World Bank (1992), *Malaysia: Forest Sector Review*, World Bank Report, Washington DC: World Bank.

6.7 Health

C   Alberini, A., Cropper, M., Fu, T.T., Krupnick, A., Liu, J.T., Shaw, D. and Harrington, W. (1995), *Valuing Health Effects of Air Pollution in Developing Countries: the Case of Taiwan*, Discussion Paper 95–01, Washington DC: Resources for the Future.

Uses contingent valuation to estimate WTP in Taiwan for avoiding illness. Finds that Taiwanese WTP around $40 to avoid an illness lasting 5.3 days and with 2.2. symptoms. This is then compared to a benefits transfer (BT) estimate in which US values for similar illnesses are adjusted by the ratio of the two income levels. Suggests that this simple BT approach works well for US and Taiwan.

C   Chemonics International and Associates (1994), *Comparing Environmental Health Risks in Cairo, Egypt, Vols 1 and 2*, Report to US AID, Egypt.

This study does not engage in monetary valuation, but amended by Pearce (1995) to suggest $350 million to $1,500 million a year health damage costs, assuming a value of statistical life taken to be $2.25 million * GNP per capita Egypt/GNP per capita USA = $62,021. Restricted Activity Days (RADs) valued at daily GNP per capita of $1.75 per day. Population taken to be 9.08 million. Estimates of hospital admissions valued at $260; minor restricted activity days and days or respiratory symptoms valued at $0.4, asthma attacks valued at $2.5. Unit values taken from Ostro (1994) on Indonesia as GNP per capita in Egypt and Indonesia is very similar.

C   Convery, F. and Tutu, K., (1993), *Estimating Gross Costs of Environmental Degradation – Sectoral Analysis: a Ghana Case Study*. Department of Economics, Dublin: University College Dublin.

Estimates additional health expenditure costs (drugs and medical expenditure) plus forgone output of environmentally related diseases in Ghana at 1.67 billion cedis, or about $5.1 million. No comment is made on this surprisingly low figure.

C   Florig, H.K. (1993), *The Benefits of Air Pollution Reduction in China*, Washington DC: Resources for the Future, mimeograph.

Finds massive impact of particulate air pollution on Chinese health and tentatively suggests damage costs may amount for 11 percent of Chinese GNP.

C   Krupnick, A., Harrison, K., Nickell, E. and Toman, M. (1993), *Assessing the Health Benefits of Improved Air Quality in Central and Eastern Europe*, Discussion Paper ENR93–19, Washington DC: Resources for the Future and in *Resources*, Fall 1993.

Assesses potential benefits of improving SO_2, particulate and lead emissions in Eastern Europe to EC levels. Mortality is valued by taking USA valuations of statistical lives and adjusting them (a) by income ratios and (b) income ratios adjusted for the income elasticity of demand. Nearly all health benefits accrue from particulate control. Low estimates of benefits are 1–4 percent of GDP and middle-range estimates are 4–12 percent.

C   Margulis, S. (1992), *Back of the Envelope Estimates of Environmental Damage Costs in Mexico*, Working Paper WPS 824, Country Department II, Latin America and the Caribbean Regional Office, Washington DC: World Bank.

Estimates annual health benefits from air pollution control of some $1 billion per annum, or around $60 per capita per annum. Value of statistical life of $75,000 assumed based on human capital approach. Population of 17 million assumed.

C   Ostro, B. (1994), *Estimating the Health Effects of Air Pollutants: a Method with an Application to Jakarta*, Policy Research Working Paper 1301, Washington DC: World Bank. See also World Bank (1994), *Indonesia Environment and Development: Challenges for the Future*, Environment Unit, Country Department III, East Asia and Pacific Region, Washington DC: World Bank.

Estimates both air and water pollution impacts on health. Assumes value of statistical life of $75,000 and population at risk of 8.2 million. Morbidity effects of air pollution include Restricted Activity Days, outpatient visits, hospital admissions, respiratory illness among children, asthma attacks and respiratory symptoms. Air pollution health damages for Jakarta come to some $220 million a year or some $27 per capita. Water pollution damages assumes 7,000 diarrhoea related deaths per year. Improved water quality and sanitation can reduce such deaths by 55–60 percent per annum, so that 3,800–4,200 deaths could be avoided. Some 360,000 less diarrhoeal episodes per year are estimated to saved by improved water quality. Economic total for water pollution is $300 million a year

C   Ostro, B., Miguel Sanchez, J., Aranda, C. and Eskeland, G. (1994), 'Air

Pollution and Mortality: Results from a Study of Santiago, Chile', submitted to *Journal of Exposure Analysis and Environmental Epidemiology*. See also World Bank (1994), *Chile: Managing Environmental Problems – Economic Analysis of Selected Issues*, Environment and Urban Development Division, Country Department I, Latin America and the Caribbean Region, Washington DC: World Bank.

Estimates are based on dose–response functions for mortality and morbidity converted to work days lost, each work day being valued at US$9.55. Population of Santiago taken to be 4.8 million. Control costs for this package of measures were estimated at $60 million, so that, even without considering other pollutants, the benefits of reduced PM_{10} exceed the costs of control. Other benefits arise form the associated control of ozone, NO_x and SO_x. Benefits from a package of reduction measures total over $100 million per annum or around $25 per capita per annum.

C   Parikh, K., Parikh, J., Muraleedharan, T. and Hadker, N. (1994), *Economic Valuation of Air Pollution in Chembur, Bombay*, Bombay: Indira Gandhi Institute of Development Research.

Uses dose–response functions for health and hedonic property model for general air pollution impacts. The dose–response function links mortality to SO_2 rather than particulate matter. Value of statistical life is estimated on the basis of human capital approach (124 million Rs); wage differentials (93 million Rs) and the implied value in the Workman's Compensation Act (69 million Rs). Work days lost are linked to particulate matter and morbidity costs are estimated using medical and hospital costs. The hedonic property price study also found links between particulate matter and rentals.

C   Pearce, D.W. (1995), 'Economic Impacts of Urban Environmental Degradation', Draft Material for *World Resources 1996–7*, Centre for Social and Economic Research on the Global Environment, London: University College London.

Reviews estimates of pollution damage costs in developed and developing countries. Suggests air pollution damages are substantial and fully justify control measures.

C   RCG Hagler Bailly Inc. (1995), *Economic Assessment of Environmental Impacts: a Workbook*, prepared for Asian Development Bank, Manila.

A workbook aimed at demonstrating how 'benefits transfer' can be used to value environmental impacts in Asian countries.

C   Seroa da Motta, R. and Fernandes Mendes A.P. (1993), *Health Costs Associated with Air Pollution in Brazil*, Rio de Janeiro: Applied Economic Research Institute, mimeograph.

Evaluates mortality response to inhalable particulate matter, sulphur dioxide, ozone, carbon monoxide, and nitrogen dioxide, using a production function approach. Ozone and particulates are strongly linked to respiratory system disease. Dose–response functions are found to predict officially ascribed deaths extremely well. Valuation was based on hospital costs and foregone output. At 5 percent discount rate costs in Sao Paulo are $2.2 million, in Cubatao $0.9 million and in Rio $0.4 million. The implicit 'values of statistical lives' are around $7,000 compared to values of $20,000 estimated by the author for water pollution.

C   Shin, E. (1994), *Economic Analysis and Valuation of Urban Environmental Problems*, Economic Department, Seoul, Korea: Yonsei University, *mimeograph*.

Highly provisional paper suggesting unit values for morbidity and mortality from air pollution in Seoul.

G   Shin, E., Gregory, R., Hufschmidt, M., Lee, Y.S., Nickum, J. and Umetsu, C., *Valuing the Economic Impacts of Environmental Problems: Asian Cities*, Urban Management Programme, Washington DC: World Bank.

Chapter 3 of this draft volume includes estimates of health effects from air pollution. Bangkok particulate pollution health damages put at $330–450 million per annum in 1989; carbon monoxide $11–27 million; lead $40–49 million, and other air toxics at $3–4 million, a total of $380–550m. Wrongly states VOSL to be the discounted value of future earnings.

C   Southgate, D. (1995), *Economic Development, Air Pollution and Public Policy: the Case of Quito, Ecuador*, Department of Agricultural Economics, Ohio State University, mimeograph.

Estimates health damage costs in Quito from particulates at some $30 million per annum or around $26 per capita per annum, which is consistent with studies of other cities.

C   World Bank (1994), *Thailand: Mitigating Pollution and Congestion Impacts in a High Growth Economy*, Country Operations Division, Country Department 1, East Asia and Pacific Region, Washington DC: World Bank.

Estimates benefits of air pollution control in Bangkok at $0.75–3 billion per annum for a 20 percent reduction in air pollution, or some $100–400 per capita per annum. Population of 7.67 million assumed. Value of statistical life of $336,000 based on compensating wage differentials in Bangkok for risky occupations.

6.8 Marine and Coastal Areas (see also wetlands)

C   Dixon, J. (1993), 'Economic Benefits of Marine Protected Areas', *Oceanus*, **36** (3), 35–40.

Looks at costs and revenues from protected marine areas in the Caribbean: Virgin Islands national park, Saba Marine Park in the Netherlands Antilles and Bonaire Marine Park. Recommends user charges.

C Dixon, J., Fallon Scura, L. and Van't Hof, T. (1994), 'Ecology and Microeconomics as 'Joint Products': the Bonaire Marine Park in the Caribbean', in Perrings, C. *et al., Biodiversity Conservation*, Amsterdam: Kluwer.

C Dixon, J. and Hodgson, G. (1988), 'Economic Evaluation of Coastal Resources: the El Nido Study', *Tropical Coastal Area Management*, August, 5–7.
    Extends Hodgson and Dixon (1988).

C Dixon, J. and Lal, P.N. (1994), 'The Management of Coastal Wetlands: Economic Analysis of Combined Ecologic–Economic Systems', in Dasgupta, P. and Maler, K.G. (eds), *The Environment and Emerging Development Issues*, Oxford: Clarendon Press.
    Surveys previous estimates of economic values for coastal wetlands.

G Dixon, J., Fallon-Scura, L. and Van't Hof, T. (1993), 'Meeting Ecological and Economic Goals: Marine Parks in the Caribbean', *Ambio*, **22** (2), 117–125.

C Fallon-Scura, L. and Van't Hof, T. (1993), *The Ecology and Economics of Bonaire Marine Park*, Environment Department, Divisional Paper 1993–44, Washington DC: World Bank.
    Assesses ecological thresholds for numbers of divers per year before coral reef damage occurs, and estimates costs and benefits of protecting the marine park.

   Gammage, S. (1994), *Estimating the Total Economic Value of a Mangrove Ecosystem in El Salvador*, Report to the UK Overseas Development Administration, London, mimeograph.
    Estimates economic values of various management strategies for El Salvador mangroves based on their value for fisheries, fuelwood, and timber. The sustainable management strategy is shown to have an economic value only slightly above that of the current strategy if discount rates are high (19 percent), but well above if the discount rate is low (8 or 5 percent).

C Georgiou, S., Söderqvist, T., Sändstrom, M. and Zylicz, T. (1995), *Baltic Sea Cleanup: Estimates of Willingness to Pay*, Centre for Social and Economic Research on the Global Environment, Working Paper, forthcoming.
    Summarises a number of contingent valuation and travel cost studies which have estimated the economic value of cleaning up eutrophication damage in the Baltic Sea region (including the former planned economies of eastern Europe). The studies mainly focus on recreation and some non-use values. A simple benefits transfer exercise is carried out to give a crude assessment of the total basin wide benefit estimate from cleanup. This indicates that the benefits may be substantial.

G   Hamilton, L., Dixon, J. and Owen Miller, G. (1989), 'Mangroves: an Undervalued Resource of the Land and of the Sea', in Borgese, E.M. *et al.*, *Ocean Yearbook 8*, Chicago: Chicago University Press.

C   Hodgson, G. and Dixon, J. (1988), 'Measuring Economic Losses due to Sediment Pollution: Logging versus Tourism and Fisheries', *Tropical Coastal Area Management*, April, 5–8.

Assesses cost of fisheries losses in Philippines due to sedimentation arising from logging. The net benefits to the combined total of logging, fishing and tourism is found to be highest when there is a hypothesised logging ban.

6.9 National Accounting (including aggregated national environmental costs)

C   Adger, W.N. (1992) 'Sustainable National Income and Natural Resource Degradation in Zimbabwe', in Turner, R.K. (ed.), *Sustainable Environmental Economics and Management: Principles and Practice*, London: Belhaven Press, pp. 338–359.

The study estimates the rents from deforestation in Zimbabwe in 1987, soil erosion in 1990 and mineral extraction for 1990–91. Given their high dependency on primary production the relevance of national accounts adjusted for resource depletion is stressed in developing countries. Figures for soil erosion show that depreciation of natural capital in 1987 was equivalent to nearly 30 percent of agricultural GDP and 5 percent of aggregate GDP. Fuelwood depreciation was 9 percent of agricultural GDP.

G   Ahmad, Y.J., El Serafy, S. and Lutz, E. (eds) (1989), *Environmental Accounting for Sustainable Development*, Washington DC: The World Bank.

C   Bartelmus, P., Lutz, E. and Schweinwest, S. (1992), *Integrated Environmental and Economic Accounting: A Case Study for Papua New Guinea*, Environment Working Paper No. 54, Washington DC: World Bank.

The study points out where problems might arise in building an SEEA (System of Environmental and Economic Accounts). Public environmental expenditure is a relatively small 0.27 percent of GDP from 1986–1990, but it is increasing and is a 0.74 percent of total government budget.

C   Crowards, T. (1994), *Natural Resource Accounting for Zimbabwe*, Centre for Social and Economic Research on the Global Environment, University College London.

Estimates rentals to woodlands, soils and minerals in Zimbabwe at 3.3 percent of GDP in 1980 and 1.7 percent in 1989. These rentals are equivalent to the value of depreciation in the relevant sectors.

C   Cruz, W. and Repetto, R. (1992), *The Environmental Effects of Stabilisation and Structural Adjustment Programs: The Philippines Case*, Washington DC: World Resources Institute.

Resource depreciation is estimated for forestry, soil erosion and coastal fisheries; combined they average 4 percent of GNP and 20 percent of gross domestic investment from 1970–1987. This was greater than external debt, increasing at a rate of 3.2 percent of GDP. The authors see this increasing liability as symptomatic of the worsening balance sheet for natural assets.

G   Hamilton, K.E. (1993), *Resource Depletion, Discoveries and Net National Product*, Centre for Social and Economic Research on the Global Environment, University College London, mimeograph.

G   Hamilton, K.E. (1992), *The Basic Identities of Environmental National Accounting*, Centre for Social and Economic Research on the Global Environment, University College London, mimeograph.

C   Hartwick, J.M. and Hageman A.P. (1991), *Economic Depreciation of Mineral Stocks and the Contribution of El Serafy*, Environment Department Working Paper No. 1991–27, Washington DC: World Bank.

C   Lallement, D. (1990), *Burkina Faso: Economic Issues in Renewable Natural Resource Management*, Sahelian Department, Washington DC: World Bank.

G   Lutz, E., Munasinghe, M. and Chander, R. (1990), *A Developing Country Perspective on Environmental Accounting*, Environment Department Working Paper 90–12, Washington DC: World Bank.

G   Lutz, E. (ed) (1993), *Toward Improved Accounting for the Environment*, Washington DC: World Bank.

G   Mäler, K.G. (1991), 'National Accounts and Environmental Resources', *Environmental and Resource Economics*, 1, 1–15.

G   Parikh, K., Parikh, J., Sharma, V.K. and Painuly, J. (1992), *Natural*
C   *Resource Accounting: a Framework for India*, Bombay: Indira Gandhi Institute of Development Research.

Sets a framework for modified income accounting for India. It includes approaches to estimating non-market sector activities as well as natural resource accounts. The report recommends an action plan based on immediate priorities. This includes assessing the physical environmental impacts of selected production and consumption activities including the informal sector, and physical accounts for soil, air, water, forests, biodiversity, and various non-renewable resources. Economic valuation should be investigated with the aim of securing integrated economic and environmental accounting.

M   Peskin, H.M. (1989b), *Accounting for Natural Resource Depletion and Degradation in Developing Countries*, Environment Department

Working Paper No. 13, Washington DC: World Bank.

Provides an adjusted account that imputes a value for the depletion of forest resources in Tanzania due to firewood collection. The value of physical depreciation of forests in Tanzania is about 5 percent of conventionally measured GDP in 1980 and considerably greater than the marketed imputation for fuelwood production in that year.

C Repetto, R., Magrath, W., Wells, M., Beer, C. and Rossini, F. (1989),
G *Wasting Assets: Natural Resources in the National Accounts*, Washington DC: World Resources Institute.

Changes in the stocks of natural resources such as oil, forests and soil for Indonesia are considered in the capital account as well as the changes in man-made capital. Optimal paths for extraction following the Hotelling Rule and the net price method is used.

C Sadoff, C.W. (1992), *The Effects of Thailand's Logging Ban: Overview and Preliminary Results*, Bangkok: Thailand Development Research Institute.

In spite of the logging ban in Thailand, deforestation continues, so environmental benefits are limited. Sadoff claims that the rates of logging in neighbouring countries have increased. A more efficient policy would be to combine sustainable management practices where logging is permitted, and a tightening of the ban elsewhere.

C Seroa Da Motta, R. and Young, C.E.F. (1991), *Natural Resources and National Accounts: Sustainable Income from Mineral Extraction*, Rio de Janeiro: Instituto de Planejamento Economico e Social.

C Seroa Da Motta, R. and May, P.H. (1992), *Loss in Forest Resource Values Due to Agricultural Land Conversion in Brazil*, Texto para Discussão No. 248, Rio de Janeiro: Instituto de Planejamento Economico e Social.

C Seroa Da Motta, R., Mendes, A.P.F., Mendes, F.E. and Young, C.E.F. (1992), *Perdas e Serviços Ambientais do Recurso Água para Uso Doméstico*, Texto Para Discussão No. 258, Rio de Janeiro: Instituto de Planejamento Economico e Social.

C Solorzano, R., de Camino, R., Woodward, R., Tosi, J., Watson, V., Vásquez, A., Villalobos, C., Jiménez, J., Repetto, R. and Cruz, W. (1991), *Accounts Overdue: Natural Resource Depreciation in Costa Rica*, Washington DC: World Resources Institute.

Focuses on forestry, soil erosion and fisheries. All expected future damages are capitalised into present values and added to the depreciation figures. The figures are deducted from the gross product of the sector to get the net product.

M United Nations (1977), *Provisional International Guidelines on the National and Sectoral Balance Sheet and Reconciliation Accounts of the System of National Accounts*, Series M, No. 60, New York: United Nations Statistical Office.

G United Nations (1990), *SNA Handbook on Integrated Environmental and*

Economic Accounting, Preliminary draft of part I: General Concepts, New York: United Nations Statistical Office.

M United Nations (1992), *Revised System of National Accounts. Chapter XXI, Satellite Analysis and Accounts*, (provisional), New York: United Nations Statistical Office.

C Van Tongeren, J., Schweinfest, S., Lutz, E., Gomez Luna M. and Guillen, F. (1991), *Integrated Environmental and Economic Accounting: A Case Study for Mexico*, Environment Working Paper No. 50, Washington DC: World Bank.

This case study is the first empirical experience with the overall analytical framework developed in the United Nations Statistical Office. The main innovation is the enlargement of the asset boundary, including oil depletion, degradation concerns, land use concerns and deforestation. The results presented in an input–output scheme show not only the macro-effects of depletion and degradation but also identify the economic use of natural resources and environmental protection expenses made by different sectors.

C Young, C.E.F. (1992), *Renda Sustentável da Indústria Extrativa no Brasil*, Rio de Janeiro: IEI/UFRJ.

6.10 Recreation and Ecotourism

C Abala, D. (1987), 'A Theoretical and Empirical Investigation of the Willingness-to-Pay for Recreational Services: A Case Study of the Nairobi National Park', *Eastern African Economics Review*, **3** (2).

The study uses the contingent valuation method to estimate the factors that influence an individual's WTP for using the Nairobi National Park. Results show that education, income, physical attributes of the park, and other factors significantly influence WTP.

C Ahmad, S., Sabri, W. and Rashid, R. (1990), Benefit Valuation of Outdoor Recreation Resources, in *Research and Publications 1988/89*, Faculty of Forestry, University Pertanian Malaysia, Serdang, Selangor, Malaysia.

The authors use the contingent valuation method to estimate the value of outdoor recreation at Semenyih Dam in Peninsular Malaysia.

C Durojaiye, B. and Ikpi, A. (1988), 'The Monetary Value of Recreational Facilities in a Developing Economy: A Case Study of Three Centres in Nigeria', *Natural Resources Journal*, **28** (2), 315–328.

The travel cost technique was used to value three recreational facilities in Nigeria. The values were significant to the economies of the two cities concerned, and much larger than the alternative land use values.

C Grandstaff, S. (1986), 'Tongonan Geothermal Power Plant Project in Leyte, Philippines', in Dixon, J. and Hufschmidt, M. (ed.), *Economic Valuation Techniques for the Environment*, London: The Johns Hopkins University

Press.

A cost-effectiveness approach was employed to choose the least costly alternative among several wastewater disposal schemes taking into account both treatment costs and environmental damage costs. By clearly defining the range of possible impacts of the alternative geothermal fluid disposal systems available, and by placing monetary values on these impacts where possible, a more informed and environmentally sensitive project design is possible.

C   Grandstaff, S. and Dixon, J. (1986), 'Evaluation of Lumpinee Park in Bangkok, Thailand', in Dixon, J. and Hufschmidt, M. (eds), *Economic Valuation Techniques for the Environment: A Case Study Workbook*, Baltimore, Maryland: John Hopkins University Press.

Lumpinee is an urban park used for short visits, as against longer trips to national parks that most studies have focused on. The travel cost method and contingent valuation were used to place a monetary value on benefits received by both park users and non-users. Estimates of users' WTP were nearly identical under the travel cost and contingent valuation approaches.

C   Maille, P. and Mendelsohn, R. (1993), 'Valuing Ecotourism in Madagascar', *Journal of Environmental Management*, **38**, 213–218.

Travel cost analysis of foreign visitors is used to determine the value per visitor of tropical biological reserves in Madagascar. The value per visitor is estimated to be between $276 and $360.

C   Mercer, D.E. and Kramer, R.A. (1992), *An International Nature Tourism Travel Cost Model: Estimating the Recreational Use Value of a Proposed National Park in Madagascar*, Presented at Association of Environmental and Resource Economists, University of New Orleans.

An international nature tourism travel cost model is derived. The model provides a conceptual framework for rigorous policy analysis of the potential nature tourism benefits accruable from allocating scarce resources to biodiversity preservation through the creation of national parks. See Kramer *et al.* (1993).

C   Moran, D. (1994), 'Contingent Valuation and Biodiversity Conservation in Kenyan Protected Areas', *Biodiversity and Conservation* (forthcoming).

A contingent valuation survey of foreign visitors to Kenyan parks and reserves. Using a discrete choice question format the survey reveals an expected mean WTP of $72 per day on the part of foreign visitors for the purpose of park maintenance.

C   Tobias, D. and Mendelsohn, R. (1991), 'Valuing Ecotourism in a Tropical Rain Forest Reserve', *Ambio*, **20**.

Estimates local WTP for visits to a forest area in Costa Rica.

Wells, M. (1993), 'Neglect of Biological Riches: The Economics of Nature

Tourism in Nepal', *Biodiversity and Conservation*, 2, 445–464.

Estimates revenues from entry to national parks in Nepal at $1 million, but cost of upkeep of parks at $5 million. Total tourist expenditures related to park visits, however, amounts to $27 million, suggesting a failure to appropriate the true revenues.

Wright, N. (1994), *An Economic Analysis of Coral Reef Production in Negril, Jamaica*, BA Thesis, Williams College, Williamstown, Massachusetts.

Uses the contingent valuation and travel cost methods to estimate visitors' consumer's surplus at Negril, Jamaica, where the coral reef is under serious threat.

The results were: WTP to conserve reef at current level: $31 per annum; WTP to improve reef to 90 percent healthy level: $49 per annum.

Valuations are differentiated by type of visitor: scuba divers are WTP $38 per annum for the current state of the reef, while those who have never seen the reef are WTP $28. The corresponding figures for an improvement in the reefs are $75 and $37.

6.11 Sanitation (see also water supply and water quality)

C   Darling, A., Gomez, C. and Niklitschek, M. (1993), 'The Question of a Public Sewerage System in a Caribbean Country: a Case Study', in Munasinghe, M. (1993), *Environmental Economics and Natural Resource Management in Developing Countries*, Committee of International Development Institutions on the Environment (CIDIE), Washington DC: World Bank.

Uses contingent valuation for the 'swimmability' of coastal waters, and risk analysis of the pollution–health link to assess the feasibility of a public sewerage system for an unnamed Caribbean island.

C   Whittington, D., Lauria, D., Wright, A., Choe, K. and Swarna, V. (1992), *Household Demand for Improved Sanitation Services: A Case Study of Kumasi, Ghana*, UNDP–World Bank Water and Sanitation Program, Washington DC: World Bank.

This contingent valuation study found that most households were willing to pay more for improved sanitation than they were currently paying but in absolute terms the potential revenues are not large, confirming that conventional sewerage is not affordable to the vast majority. On the other hand improved ventilated pit latrines, which are much cheaper, would need only modest government subsidies.

C   Whittington, D., Lauria, D., Wright, A., Choe, K., Hughes, J. and Swarna, V. (1993), 'Household Demand for Improved Sanitation Services in Kumasi, Ghana', *Water Resources Research*, 29 (6), 1539–1560.

A contingent valuation study was conducted to estimate households'

WTP for two types of improved sanitation services: improved ventilated pit latrines and water closets connected to a sewer system. Most households were willing to pay more for improved sanitation than they were currently paying for the existing sanitation system (mostly public and bucket latrines), but potential revenues from households are not large. The study confirms the view that conventional sewerage systems are not affordable to the vast majority of households without massive government subsidies. However, only modest subsidies are required for on-site sanitation (ventilated pit latrines): WTP is about as high as it is for water closets, and ventilated pit latrines are much cheaper to supply.

C   Whittington, D., Lauria, D., Wright, A., Choe, K., Hughes, J. and Swarna, V. (1993), 'Household Sanitation in Kumasi, Ghana: a Description of Current practices, Attitudes and Perceptions', *World Development*, 21 (5), 733–748.

A survey of 1,200 households in Kumasi revealed a dangerous public health risk from the existing sanitation system. Only 10 percent of generated human waste is removed from the city. Expenditure on sanitation services was only $1.50 per capita per year and, correspondingly, households were getting very poor service. Households were quite open to the idea of simple, low cost, on-site solutions to their sanitation problems.

6.12 Soil Erosion and Land Degradation

G   Bishop, J. (1992), *Economic Analysis of Soil Degradation*, London Environmental Economics Centre, Gatekeeper Series 92–01, London.

C   Bishop, J. (1990), *The Cost of Soil Erosion in Malawi*, Consultant Report, Country Operations Division, Southern Africa Department, Washington DC: World Bank.

The study finds a link between soil loss and crop yields. Economic losses are about 4 percent to 26 percent of composite net farm income for Malawi as a whole.

C   Bishop, J. and Allen, J. (1989), *The On-Site Costs of Soil Erosion in Mali*, Environment Department Working Paper No. 21, Washington DC: World Bank.

For Malawi as a whole, the study estimates a mean current rate of soil erosion of 20 tonnes/hectare/year on gross arable land. The on-site cost of soil erosion is expressed in terms of reduced crop yields, resulting in mean annual yield losses between 4 percent and 25 percent. For Mali, gross annual losses are estimated to be between 0.5 percent and 3.1 percent of 1988 GDP.

C   Bojö, J. (1986), 'Cost–Benefit Studies of Soil and Water Conservation Projects: a Review of 20 Empirical Studies', in K. Tato and H. Hurni (eds) (1992), *Soil Conservation for Survival*, Iowa: Soil and Water Conservation Society (7515 Northeast Ankeny Road, Iowa, 50021–9764).

The purpose of this paper is to shed some light on the extent to which theoretical cost–benefit analysis has been applied to soil and water conservation projects, what the major difficulties have been, and what policy conclusions can be derived from those experiences.

G   Bojö, J. (1990), *The Economics of Land Degradation: Theory and*
C   *Applications to Lesotho*, Published Ph.D. dissertation, EFI, Stockholm School of Economics, Box 6501, 113 83, Stockholm.

Bojö, J. and Cassells, D. (1995), *Land Degradation and Rehabilitation in Ethiopia: a Reassessment*, AFTES Working Paper No. 17, Washington DC: World Bank.

Makes allowance for re-deposition of eroded soil to estimate net costs of land degradation to Ethiopia. The resulting soil erosion cost is small at $2 million, but the costs of nutrient losses due to the practice of burning dung and crop residues rather than using them to restore soil fertility are estimated at $100 million.

C   Convery, F. and Tutu, K. (1993), *Estimating Gross Costs of Environmental Degradation – Sectoral Analysis: a Ghana Case Study*, Department of Economics, University College Dublin.

Estimates, very approximately, the costs of lost soil nutrients due to land degradation in Ghana. A figure of $80 million is suggested for crop loss and $8.4 million for reduced livestock production due to nutrient loss.

C   Cruz, W., Francisco, H. and Conway, Z. (1988), 'The On-Site and Downstream Costs of Soil Erosion in the Magat and Pantabangan Watersheds', *Journal of Philippine Development*, 15 (1).

C   Fleming, W. (1983), 'Phewa Tal Catchment Program: Benefits and Costs of Forestry and Soil Conservation in Nepal', in Hamilton, L.S. (ed.), *Forest and Watershed Development and Conservation in Asia and the Pacific*, Boulder: Westview Press.

C   Golan, E.H. (1992), *Soil Conservation and Sustainable Development in the Sahel: a Study of Two Senegalese Villages*, World Employment Programme, Working Paper WEP 2–22/WP.235, Geneva: International Labour Organisation.

Applies a micro (community level) Social Accounting Matrix to simulate crop choice, soil conservation effort and income effects of alternative tax/subsidy schemes on an erosive crop (groundnuts) and other conservation interventions.

C   Grohs, F. (1992), *Monetarising (sic) Environmental Damages: a Tool for Development Planning? A Case Study of Soil Erosion in Zimbabwe*, Paper presented to International Society for Ecological Economics Conference, Stockholm. See Grohs (1993).

C   Grohs, F. (1993), *Economics of Soil Degradation, Erosion and*

Conservation: a Case Study of Zimbabwe, Ph.D. Thesis, University of Hohenheim, Stuttgart.

Assesses the economic costs of soil erosion to small-holder farmers in Zimbabwe through the productivity loss approach. The methodology uses the Soil Loss Estimation Method for Southern Africa (SLEMSA) for field level estimation, and a GIS aggregation for aggregate costs. Off-site costs in small dams are estimated. The results suggests a high 3 percent yield decline per 1 centimetre of soil lost; smallholder farm income losses for 1989 of $Z 4.4 million, and $Z 1.7 million losses for the large scale sector. These are considerably below those estimated by Stocking (see Stocking, 1986).

C   Hodgson, G. and Dixon, J. (1988), *Logging versus Fisheries and Tourism in Palawan*, Occasional Paper No. 7, Hawaii: East–West Centre.

C   Kim, S.H. and Dixon, J. (1986), 'Economic Valuation of Environmental Quality Aspects of the Upland Agricultural Projects in Korea', in Dixon, J. and Hufschmidt, M. (eds), *Economic Valuation Techniques for the Environment*, Baltimore: The Johns Hopkins University Press.

C   Knowler, D. (1993), *Economics and Planning for Improved Land management: Two Cases from West Africa*. Unpublished manuscript Rome: Food and Agricultural Organisation Investment Centre.

Uses change of productivity approach to estimate the cost of soil erosion in Ghana and Nigeria.

G   Lutz, E., Pagiola, S. and Reiche, C. (eds), (forthcoming), *Economic and Institutional Analyses of Soil Conservation Projects in Central America and the Caribbean*, Environment Department Working Paper, Washington DC: World Bank.

C   Lutz, E., Pagiola, S. and Reiche, C. (1994), *Cost–Benefit Analysis of Soil Conservation in Central America and the Caribbean*, World Bank Environment Paper No. 8, Washington DC: World Bank, and *World Bank Research Observer*.

Estimates yield losses due to soil erosion in various areas of Central America and the Caribbean. The edited volume consist of 18 chapters on various issues relating to soil erosion. Damage cost studies are summarised by the editors. Rates of return to soil conservation measures range from 16–84 percent (with two exceptions of negative rates of return), Measured against high private discount rates the effects are varied with some schemes having very short pay-back periods and others have very long pay-back periods. As the authors note: 'these results of the economic analysis suggest that it can be perfectly rational for farmers not to adopt proposed conservation measures'.

C   Margulis, S. (1992), *Back-of-the-Envelope Estimates of Environmental Damage Costs in Mexico*, Working Paper, Washington DC: World Bank.

For developing countries that may not be able to afford in-depth study of every environmental issue, rough estimates of economic costs of various environmental problems are needed to help rank the issues. Valuation methods are presented along with their limitations. Some damages such as the loss of biodiversity are however too complex and are not quantified.

C   Magrath, W. and Arens, P. (1989), *The Costs of Soil Erosion on Java: A Natural Resource Accounting Approach*, Environmental Department Working Paper 15, Washington DC: World Bank.

C   Norse, D and Saigal, R. (1993), 'National Economic Cost of Soil Erosion in Zimbabwe', in Munasinghe, M. (ed.), *Environmental Economics and Natural Resource Management in Developing Countries*, Committee of International Development Institutions on the Environment (CIDIE), Washington DC: World Bank.

Uses replacement costs of fertiliser to value soil loss in Zimbabwe and estimates annual cost to be $150 million on arable lands alone, or 13–60 percent of the gross returns per hectare.

M   Pagiola, S. (forthcoming), 'Cost Benefit Analysis of Soil Conservation', in Lutz, E., Pagiola, S. and Reider, C. (eds) (forthcoming), *Economic and Institutional Analyses of Soil Conservation Projects in Central America and the Caribbean*, Environment Department Working Paper, Washington DC : World Bank.

C   Pol, F. van der (1992), *Soil Mining: An Unseen Contributor to Farm Income in Southern Mali*, Royal Tropical Institute Bulletin 325, Amsterdam.

Uses a nutrient loss approach to value soil degradation in southern Mali.

C   Shah, P., Schreier, H., Browns, S. and Riley, K. (1991), *Soil Fertility and Erosion Issues in the Middle Mountains of Nepal*, Workshop Proceedings, Jhikhu Khola Watershed, sponsored by the International Development Research Centre, Ottawa, Canada.

This workshop discusses the results of research on the Middle Mountains of Nepal, monitoring the resources dynamics in the region. The aim is to integrate this work, to understand the resource problems of the Middle Mountains, identify research priorities, determine appropriate avenues for implementation of policies and gain feedback for the next phase of the Jhikhu Khola Soil Fertility and Erosion Research Project.

C   Stocking, M. (1986), *The Cost of Soil Erosion in Zimbabwe in Terms of the Loss of Three Major Nutrients*, Consultants' Working Paper No. 3, Rome: Food and Agriculture Organisation.

Replacement costs of soil erosion in Zimbabwe are estimated at up to $Z1.5 billion, based on erosion estimates from the Universal Soil Loss Equation Model (USLE), These estimates are more than double the value of net agricultural output in the same year.

C   Veloz, A., Southgate, D., Hitzhusen, F. and Macgregor, R. (1985), 'The Economics of Erosion Control in a Subtropical Watershed: a Dominican Case', *Land Economics*, 61 (2).

6.13 Solid Waste Management

Gutman, P. (1994), *Reynosa Municipal Solid Waste Disposal Alternatives*, Washington DC: World Bank, mimeograph.

Analyses waste collection and disposal in Reynosa, Mexico and makes tentative estimates of some of the health costs.

Pearce, D.W. and Turner, R.K. (1994), *Economics and Solid Waste Management in the Developing World*, Working Paper 94–05, Centre for Social and Economic Research on the Global Environment, University College London and University of East Anglia, UK.

Surveys economics of waste disposal in LDCs. Notes consensus estimates on waste disposal costs and some very limited evidence on costs of health hazards from inefficient collection and disposal in Mexico, and costs of clean up of streets due to poor collection in other countries.

Tin, A.M., Wise, D., Su, W.H., Reutergardh, L. and Lee, S.K. (1995), 'Cost–Benefit Analysis of the Municipal Solid Waste Collection System in Yangon, Myanmar', *Resources, Conservation and Recycling*, **14**, 103–131.

Appraisal of alternative management regimes for collecting and disposing of solid waste in the former Rangoon. While using the title 'cost benefit' the analysis covers only limited aspects of a benefit study: avoided disposal costs from more efficient systems, and increases in employment. Reductions in uncollected waste are correctly identified as an environmental health benefit, but the benefit is not measured. Increased collection involves increased truck pollution but this is not identified as an offsetting environmental cost.

6.14 Statistical Life

See under Health for Parikh *et al.*, and da Motta.

6.15 Water Supply (see also water quality, sanitation)

C   Altaf, M.A., Jamal, H. and Whittington, D. (1992), *Willingness to Pay for Water in Rural Punjab, Pakistan*, UNDP–World Bank Water and Sanitation Program, Water and Sanitation Report No. 4, Washington DC: World Bank.

The study aimed at determining the willingness of households to pay for improved service levels, the determinants of WTP, preferences regarding the management of water delivery systems, and the appropriateness of existing government policy on the provision of water in rural areas.

C   Altaf, M.A., Whittington, D., Jamal, H. and Smith, V.K. (1993),

'Rethinking Rural Water Supply Policy in the Punjab, Pakistan', *Water Resources Research*, **29** (7), 1943–1954.

Analyses public policy on rural water supply in the Punjab, Pakistan. Using household survey data, it shows that policies have not kept pace with rapid economic development. In the absence of adequate public investment, households find private sector alternatives for their water needs, often at high economic and environmental cost. Contingent valuation results indicate that household WTP for water supply is much higher than generally assumed. Full cost recovery is shown to be quite feasible in many areas.

C Boadu, F. (1992), 'Contingent Valuation for Household Water in Rural Ghana', *Journal of Agricultural Economics*, **43**.

C Briscoe, J., Castro, P., Griffin, C., North, J. and Oslen, O. (1990), 'Towards Equitable and Sustainable Rural Water Supplies: A Contingent Valuation Study in Brazil', *The World Bank Economic Review*, **4** (2).

The study shows that surveys of actual and hypothetical water-use practices can provide policy relevant information on WTP, varying according to household socioeconomic characteristics, and the characteristics of the existing and new supplies of water. In rural Brazil, tariffs for yard taps can be increased substantially before significant number of households would choose not to connect to an improved system, whereas provision of free water at public taps can protect the poor without jeopardising the financial viability of the scheme.

C Lovei, L. and Whittington, D. (1993), 'Rent-Extracting Behaviour by Multiple Agents in the Provision of Municipal Water Supply: A Study in Jakarta, Indonesia', *Water Resources Research*, **29** (7), 1965–1974.

A framework is presented for the analysis of rent-extracting behaviour by multiple agents involved in the provision of municipal water supplies in Jakarta, Indonesia. It is shown that such behaviour can dramatically affect the terms and conditions under which water service is offered to the public. A water supply system based on limited numbers of public taps, relatively few house connections, and water vendors can generate substantial monopoly rents that can be appropriated by both public and private agents. Rather than serving the public interest, agents involved in the water delivery system may pursue strategies designed for private gain which can have important and pervasive implications for how a water system is actually designed and operated.

C MacRae, D. and Whittington, D. (1988), 'Assessing Preferences in Cost–Benefit Analysis: Reflection on Rural Water Supply Evaluation in Haiti', *Journal of Policy Analysis and Management*, **7**.

This article examines an area of cost–benefit methodology which has come under increasing philosophical scrutiny in recent years: the appropriate treatment of individuals' preferences. The authors illustrate some of these problems using a concrete example: the evaluation of a rural water supply project in southern Haiti.

C   Mu, X., Whittington, D. and Briscoe, J. (1990), 'Modelling Village Water Demand Behaviour: A Discrete Choice Approach', *Water Resources Research*, **26**.

Presents a discrete choice model of householders' water source choice decisions in developing countries. The model is estimated with data from 69 households in Ukunda, Kenya, a small town south of Mombasa. The results suggest that source choices are influenced by the time it takes to collect water from different sources, the price of water, and the number of women in the household. Household income did not, however, have a statistically significant effect. The same data were used to estimate a traditional model of household demand. The results of the discrete choice and traditional models are then compared.

G   Munasinghe, M. (1990), *Managing Water Resources to Avoid Environmental Degradation*, World Bank Environment Department Working Paper No. 41, Washington, DC: World Bank.

C   North, J. and Griffin, C. (1993), 'Water Source as a Housing Characteristic: Hedonic Property Valuation and Willingness to Pay for Water', *Water Resources Research*, July.

The study estimates the determinants of the rental value of dwellings using the bid-rent approach to the hedonic price model with data from a region in the Philippines. The study finds that most households value an in-house piped water source highly, relative to other attributes. Middle- and high-income households value a deep well or piped water in the yard although less than piped water in the house. Somewhat surprisingly, households appear to gain little from having a communal source of water closer to their homes.

M   Paul, J. and Manskopf, J. (1991), *Cost-of-Illness Methodologies for Water-Related Diseases in Developing Countries*, Water and Sanitation for Health Project, Technical Report No. 75.

The report develops a methodology for the use of the cost-of-illness approach for water related projects in developing countries with a focus on potential health benefits from water supply and sanitation interventions, taking into account potential direct cost savings in the form of productivity gain in a population no longer affected by the disease or illness.

C   Seroa da Motta, R., Filho, G., Mendes, F. and Nascimento, C., *Current Status of Water Pollution Control in Brazil*, Research Institute of Applied Economics, Rio de Janeiro: Instituto de Planejamento Economico e Social.

This paper attempts to discern the effectiveness of abatement policy and the status of current water quality in Brazil. It presents the results of a study on indicators of water quality for 13 states where systematic monitoring is undertaken. A regional, sectoral and sustainability analysis of water quality and policy are also presented.

C   Singh, B., Ramasubban, R., Bhatia, R., Briscoe, J., Griffin, C. and Kim, C. (1993), 'Rural Water Supply in Kerala, India: How to Emerge from a Low-Level Equilibrium Trap', *Water Resources Research*, July.

Discusses the problems faced by rural water systems in India in particular, and in the developing world in general. The analysis suggests that it is indeed possible for the system to rise out of its current trap. The study traces out a 'new' path for water supply planners involving a few but critical policy changes; for example the critical ingredient is perceptions about the financing and purpose of public water supply systems.

C   Whittington, D., Lauria, D. and Mu, X. (1991), 'Paying for Urban Services: A Study of Water Vending and Willingness to Pay for Water in Onitsha, Nigeria', *World Development*, 19.

Discusses many of the questions involved with third world water supply systems: where the water comes from; how much households get; what uses the water is put to; how much households pay for water; and how much they would be willing to pay for improved water services. The lack of data on water demand appears to be one of the causes of the wide gap between expectations and accomplishments of urban water schemes.

C   Whittington, D., Mu, X. and Roche, R. (1990), 'Calculating the Value of Time Spent Collecting Water: Some Estimates for Ukunda, Kenya', *World Development*, 18.

Two procedures for estimating the value of time spent collecting water in developing countries are presented to derive estimates of the value of time for household in Ukunda. The value of time is high, suggesting that the economic benefit of improved water services in developing countries may be much higher than is commonly realised.

C   Whittington, D. (1989), *Water Vending and Development: Lessons from Two Countries*, USAID Water and Sanitation for Health Project, Washington DC.

C   Whittington, D., Okorafor, A., Okore, A. and McPhail, A. (1989), 'Strategy for Cost Recovery in Rural Water Sector: A Case Study of Nsukka District, Anambra State, Nigeria', *Water Resources Research*, 26 (9), 1899–1913.

In-depth interviews were conducted with 395 households in three rural communities in Nsukka district of Anambra State, Nigeria, concerning their household water use practices, water expenditures to vendors, WTP for improved water supplies, and household socioeconomic characteristics. Since households are shown not to want to pay for water in advance, nor to make fixed monthly payments, a system involving payment for water actually received when it is wanted is required. Householders did not trust government to supply such a service. Kiosk systems, or kiosks with metered private connections to some households, are the most promising way to improve cost recovery and meet consumers' cash flow needs.

C   Whittington, D., Briscoe, J., Mu, X. and Barron, W. (1990), 'Estimating the Willingness to Pay for Water Services in Developing Countries: A Case Study of the Use of Contingent Valuation Survey in Southern Haiti', *Economic Development and Cultural Change*, **38** (2).

The results of the study suggest that it is possible to carry out a contingent valuation survey among a very poor, illiterate population and still obtain reasonable and consistent answers.

C   Whittington, D., Mujwahuzi, M., McMahon, G. and Choe, K. (1988), *Willingness to Pay for Water in Newala District, Tanzania: Strategies for Cost Recovery*, Water and Sanitation for Health Project Field Report No. 246, Washington DC: USAID.

The paper presents a case study of a water planning problem in the Newala District which collapsed when diesel necessary to run the pumping station could not be provided. The aim of the WASH study was to estimate the willingness of households to pay to keep the system running, so as to save themselves the hours of waiting to collect water from traditional sources.

C   Whittington, D., Smith, K., Okorafor, A., Okore, A., Liu, J. and McPhail, A. (1991), 'Giving Respondents Time to Think in Contingent Valuation Studies: A Developing Country Application', *Journal of Environmental Economics and Management*, **22**.

A study was conducted in Nigeria as part of an evaluation of rural households' WTP for public taps and private connections to improve drinking water systems. It finds that respondents who were allowed time to evaluate the proposed water system bid significantly less than those who do not have that time. Moreover, this conclusion held for both public taps as well as private connections.

G   Whittington, D. and Choe, K. (1992), *Economic Benefits Available from the Provision of Improved Potable Water Supplies: a Review and Assessment of Existing Evidence*, prepared for Water and Sanitation for Health Project, Washington DC: US Agency for International Development.

This report summarises the existing literature on the economic benefits of potable water supplies in developing countries, price elasticities of demand for water, and households' WTP for improved water supplies.

6.16 Water Quality (see also sanitation)

C   Choe, K., Whittington, D. and Lauria, D. (1994), *The Economic Benefits of Surface Water Quality Improvements in Developing Countries: a Case Study of Davao, Philippines,* Environment Department, Washington DC: World Bank, mimeograph.

A study of WTP for improving water quality in Davao City, Philippines. Uses Contingent Valuation. WTP results: at 50 pesos ($2) per month, 25 percent of households would vote for the improvement. At 25 pesos, 50 percent would vote yes. These WTP estimates correspond to 1 percent and 0.5 percent of monthly incomes, suggesting a very low WTP for improved quality.

C   Darling, A., Gomez, C. and Niklitschek, M. (1993), 'The Question of a Public Sewerage System in a Caribbean Country: a Case Study', in Munasinghe, M. (1993), *Environmental Economics and Natural Resource Management in Developing Countries,* Committee of International Development Institutions on the Environment (CIDIE), Washington DC: World Bank.

C   McConnell, K. and Ducci, J. (1989), *Valuing Environmental Quality in Developing Countries: Two Case Studies,* Paper presented to Applied Social Science Association, Atlanta, Georgia.

Methodology: Contingent Valuation – WTP to improve sewer system to reduce coastal pollution. WTP = $11 per annum for those outside the sewer system but who could be connected, and $178 per annum for those in the sewer system. Those inside stood to gain more than those outside the sewer system because of direct access to beaches. For Montevideo used a Contingent Valuation of sewer lines to reduce contaminated beaches and water. WTP = $14 per annum, or less than 1 percent of median family income.

G   Munasinghe, M. (1990), *Managing Water Resource to Avoid Environmental Degradation,* Environment Department, Working Paper No. 41, Washington DC: World Bank.

C   Seroa da Motta, R. (1995), *Water Quality and Policy in Brazil: Estimates of Health Costs Associated to Sanitation Services and Simulation of Pollution Taxes Applied in River Basins,* Rio de Janeiro, Brazil: Instituto de Pequisa Econômica Aplicada.

Estimates the relationship between investment in sanitation and reductions in mortality from waterborne disease. Thus, extending coverage of public water supply by 1 percent of those currently without access to such a source would decrease under-14 mortality cases by 2.5 percent. For sewage collection and treatment the relevant elasticities are 1.6 percent and 2.1 percent. Rather than use a Value of Statistical Life (VOSL), the author estimates the cost of saving a life. For water supply, it is $115,000; sewage collection $214,000 and for sewage treatment it is $175,000. If all investments are engaged in simultaneously, the costs per life saved is $164,000.

6.17 Wetlands

C .Adams, W.M. and Hollis, G.E. (1989), *Hydrology and Sustainable Resource Development of Sahelian Floodplain Wetland*, Prepared for Hadejia–Nguru Wetlands Conservation Project, Nguru, Nigeria.

C Aglionby, J. (1993), *Determining the Optimal Size of a Small Scale Wetland Development Project in the Light of Environmental Costs: a Case Study at Fete, Ghana*, Centre for Social and Economic Research on the Global Environment, University College London, mimeograph.

> Develops a 'rapid appraisal' methodology for the valuation of the environmental impacts of small scale wetlands development projects in Ghana. The valuation is used to determine the optimal scale of the development.

C Barbier, E. (1993), 'Sustainable Use of Wetlands Valuing Tropical Wetland
G Benefits: Economic Methodologies and Applications', *The Geographical Journal*, **159**.

> The paper points out the importance of economic valuation of tropical wetlands and natural systems in economic development decisions. Consequences of not assessing economic impacts could often be irreversible, and borne by economies that can least afford them. A general methodological approach for valuing wetland benefits is described and fits neatly into the cost–benefit approach that can be used to analyse development policies and investments.

G Barbier, E. (1992), *Valuing Environmental Function: Tropical Wetlands*, London Environmental Economics Centre Discussion Paper 92–04.

G Barbier, E., Costanza, R. and Twilley, R. (1991), *Guidelines for Tropical Wetland Evaluation*. Report for CATIE, Turrialba, Costa Rica.

C Barbier, E., Adams, W. and Kimmage, K. (1991), *Economic Evaluation of Wetland Benefits: The Hadejia–Jama'are Floodplain, Nigeria*, London Environmental Economics Centre Discussion Paper 91–02.

> The floodplain possesses substantial economic value given its multi-faceted functions. The paper concludes that water developments that divert water from the wetlands should not proceed unless it can be demonstrated that the net benefits gained from these developments exceed the net benefits forgone through wetland loss in the floodplain.

G Barbier, E. (1989a), *The Economic Value of Ecosystems: 1 – Tropical Wetlands*, London Environmental Economics Centre Gatekeeper Series No. GK89–02.

G Barbier, E. (1989b), *Economic Evaluation of Tropical Wetland Resources:*

Applications in Central America. Prepared for International Union for the Conservation of Nature and CATIE, London Environmental Economics Centre Discussion Paper, London.

C   Dixon, J. and Lal, P.N. (1994), 'The Management of Coastal Wetlands: Economic Analysis of Combined Ecologic–Economic Systems', in Dasgupta, P. and Maler, K.G. (eds), *The Environment and Emerging Development Issues,* Oxford: Clarendon Press.

Surveys previous estimates of economic values for coastal wetlands in Thailand, Indonesia, Fiji, Malaysia and Ecuador.

G   Maltby, E. (1986), *Waterlogged Wealth: Why Waste the World's Wet Places?* London: Earthscan Publications.

C   Ruitenbeek, H.J. (1992), *Mangrove Management: An Economic Analysis of Management Options with a Focus on Bintuni Bay, Irian Jaya,* Environmental Management Development in Indonesia Project, Environmental Report No. 8.

The analysis shows that strong economic arguments exist for conservative mangrove clearing. Where strong ecological linkages occur, severe restrictions on clearing activities will prove economically optimal. Where ecosystem dynamics are uncertain, programmes reducing linkage effects will minimise potential economic losses.

C   Thomas, D., Ayache, F. and Hollis, T. (1990), 'Use Values and Non-Use Values in the Conservation of Ichkeul National Park, Tunisia', *Environmental Conservation,* **18,** 120–130.

Shows that the economic gains from taking measures to prevent the degradation of the Ichkeul National Park by releases of water from the dams outweigh the economic benefits from the use of water in agricultural irrigation.

G   Turner, R.K. (1991), 'Economics and Wetland Management', *Ambio* **20** (2).

G   Turner, R.K. and Jones, T. (1991), *Wetlands: Market and Intervention Failures,* London: Earthscan Publications.

Index